VOCABULARY
FOR THE
WORLD
OF
WORK
1
Basic Job Words

ISBN# 0-87694-229-X   EDI 383

by Donn Mosenfelder

EDUCATIONAL DESIGN, INC. EDI 383

Table of Contents

1
GETTING A JOB

Words in this chapter:

employer
employee
personnel office
job opening
job listing
job applicant
private employment agency
fee
fee paid
work study program
placement office
JTPA
WIN
State Employment Service (SES)
help wanted ads
want ads
classified ads
apply for a job
job application form
resume

cover letter
Social Security
Social Security benefit
Social Security number
work permit
work experience
marital status
dependents
references
job history
current job — former job
last job — previous jobs
immediate supervisor
job title
termination — terminated
citizenship
bonded
convicted of a felony
bondable
specify

A Where Do You Find a Job?

Do you know some **employers** you might want to work for? Call them up. Or walk in off the street. Ask if there is a **personnel office.** The personnel office will tell you if there are any **job openings.**

Applying directly to an employer is a good way to get a job. Many **job applicants** get jobs this way.

employer. The person, place, or company that you, as an **employee** (see below), work for.

employee. Job holder. Worker. An **employee** is a person who works for an **employer.**

personnel office. The part of a big company that handles hiring. It also keeps records of employees and handles some of their problems on the job.

job opening (or **listing**). Available job. A new job, or a job someone left which is now "open."

job applicant. A person who is looking for a job.

Questions

1. Ellen Jones is looking for a job. She calls the XYZ Company. She is told that the company has a job available for someone as a salesperson.

Match.

__ Ellen Jones   **A.** job opening

__ salesperson   **B.** job applicant

2. Ellen applies for the job. She goes in to talk to Ms. Bonita, who is in charge of hiring people for the XYZ Company.

Ms. Bonita works in the _____ office of the XYZ Company. (Fill in the blank.)

3. Ellen gets the job.

Match.

__ Ellen   **A.** employer

__ XYZ Company   **B.** employee

◆

A **private employment agency** may be able to help you get a job. A private agency works for money. If it gets you a job, it will probably charge you a **fee.** But if the job is **"fee paid,"** it will charge the employer.

private employment agency. A company that gets jobs for people.

fee. Money the agency charges to get you a job.

fee paid. When the job is "fee paid," the employer pays the agency's fee. You don't have to pay anything.

Questions

1. The Myron Agency gets Andrew Porter a job at the Simpson Co. The job is "fee paid." Who pays the Myron Agency's fee?

   __ **A.** Andrew Porter
   __ **B.** The Simpson Co.

2. If the job is *not* fee paid, who will pay the Myron Agency's fee?

   __ **A.** Andrew Porter
   __ **B.** The Simpson Co.

Are you in school or in a special *work study program?* Schools often have *placement offices* to help people find jobs. So do such programs as *JTPA* or *WIN.* And the *State Employment Service* is always ready to help.

All of these government services are *free!*

work study program. Designed to train students by giving them schooling plus experience on the job.

placement office. Gets people jobs.

JTPA. Stands for Job Training Partnership Act. JTPA programs get U.S. Government money to help needy people learn job skills. There are many types of JTPA programs Some help young people get jobs in the summer. Others work with people over a longer period of time to develop their skills.

WIN. Work Incentive program. Trains people who are on welfare to help them get jobs.

State Employment Service (SES). One of the best places to get jobs. And like all other government programs, it's free! Look it up in the phone book. First find the name of your state. Then look for "Labor Department."

Questions

1. Which of the following jobs is free? (You won't have to pay a fee to get it.)

   __ **A.** You get it through SES
   __ **B.** A summer job you get through JTPA
   __ **C.** The Myron Agency gets it for you, and it's *not* fee paid

2. Match.

   __ One of its programs is   **A.** JTPA
       a summer youth program   **B.** WIN
   __ Program for people on welfare

3. "Job listings" means about the same as —

__ **A.** Job applicants

__ **B.** Job openings

Your local newspaper lists job openings. These listings are called —

> **help wanted ads.** Or simply —
>
> **want ads.** Or —
>
> **classified ads.**

Want ads and *classified ads* mean the same thing. They are for things for sale, or apartments for rent — and also for jobs. The *want ads* for jobs are the *help wanted ads.* They look like this:

Questions

1. Where can you find job listings? Check all the ones that are correct.

__ **A.** employment agency

__ **B.** help wanted ads

__ **C.** placement office

__ **D.** State Employment Service

2. Match.

__ charges fee   **A.** private employment agency

__ free   **B.** SES

Review

1. Match.

___ available job   **A.** job applicant

___ person who wants   **B.** job opening
      a job

2. Match.

___ company you work for   **A.** employee

___ job holder   **B.** employer

3. You find ads like these in a newspaper.

Help Wanted 2600	Help Wanted 2600
MEDICAL ASST & SECY -for OB/ GYN, mature & experienced only need apply . Salary negotiable, excellent hours. Park area. 475-5311	MESSENGER-FULL TIME Exp'd or college student preferred for midtown business office. $4.00 per hour Apply Thursday Bell, 330 W. 23rd Fl 212-947-7600
MESSENGER **COURIERS NEEDED** Clean Driver's License. Must speak Spanish & English. Company car provided. Must be available for 2 day monthly trips to Puerto Rico. All benefits. Salary $375 weekly. Apply in person Suite 1305, 76 Beaver St. 10 a.m.-4 p.m. Jan 3, 4, 7, 8	**MESSENGERS** Full & P/T. 2 W. 46 St, Room 20 **NEWSPAPER DELIVERER** P/T or F/T, EARLY HOURS, driver's license req. Midtown loca. 689-4070

What are they called?

H__ __ __ W__ __ __ __ __ A__ __

4. A private employment agency lists a job as fee paid.

   Who pays the fee?

   ___ **A.** employer

   ___ **B.** job applicant

5. You want to apply for a job in a big company. You will probable have to apply at the pe__ __ __ __ __el office.

B Applying for a Job

Let's say you are a *job applicant.* You *apply* for a job. You will probably have to fill out a *job application form.*

> **job applicant**
>
> **apply** for a job
>
> **job application form**

You learned on page 4 what a *job applicant* is. If you don't know what the rest of these words mean, you can easily figure them out.

Question

1. Match.

    A. job applicant

    B. applying

    C. application form

---◆---

Some people write up *resumes* to tell employers what kinds of experience and background they have for job openings. A resume tells mainly about the jobs you've had and the schools you've gone to.

A resume (pronounced RAY-zoo-may) should be —

> *neat*
>
> *typed* (if it's handwritten it won't be as neat)
>
> *short* (it's best if it's on just one page)

Question

1. Here is Laura's resume. Check the good things about it.

__ **A.** neat

__ **B.** typed

__ **C.** short enough

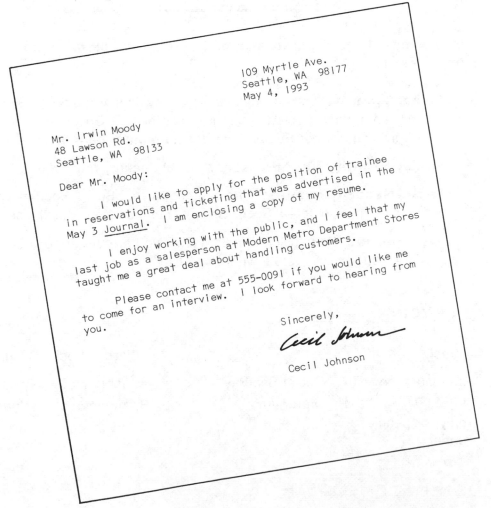

Cecil Johnson answered a help wanted ad. The ad told him to send in a resume. When Cecil sent it in he included a *cover letter* to explain what ad he was answering.

Below is his cover letter.

Questions

1. Match.

___ lists jobs and schooling you've had   **A.** cover letter

___ mentions the job you're applying for   **B.** resume

2. Should a resume be typed?

___ yes   ___ no

Should a cover letter be typed?

___ yes   ___ no

Every job holder needs a *Social Security card*. It looks like this.

If you are under 16 years old you may also need a *work permit*. Work permits are different in different states.

Social Security. You and your employer pay money into Social Security every time you get a paycheck. Social Security is run by the U.S. Government. When you get old and retire you will get *Social Security retirement benefits.*

Social Security benefit. Money Social Security pays you.

Social Security number. The number on your Social Security card. Every working person has a different Social Security number. You keep the same number always.

work permit. Permission to hold a job if you are under 16 years old. Work permits are issued by the state where you live.

Questions

1. Match.

___ an insurance program   **A.** Social Security

___ only for people under 16   **B.** work permit

2. What's a Social Security benefit?

___ **A.** money you pay in

___ **B.** money you get back

3. You lose your Social Security card. When you apply for your new card, what number will it have?

___ **A.** same

___ **B.** different

4. Where do you get a Social Security number?

___ **A.** at a store

___ **B.** from the government

___ **C.** from your boss

5. Work permit.

___ **A.** everyone needs one

___ **B.** it means you're hired

___ **C.** you may need it when you're young

◆

Let's say you see a *classified ad* for a job you want. The ad tells you to send in your *resume.* The ad gives the address of a *private employment agency.* It says the job is *fee paid.*

classified ad.

resume.

private employment agency.

fee paid.

You have seen all of these words before. What do they mean?

Questions

1. *Classified ad* means the same as W __ __ __ ad.

You find classified ads in your local __ __ __ __ __ __ __ __ __.

2. Match.

___ private employment agency   **A.** has job listings, *charges fee*

___ State Employment Service   **B.** has job listings, *does not* charge fee

3. *Application forms* and *resumes* both tell about what jobs you've had, what schools you've gone to, and so on.

What's the difference? (Match.)

___ application form

___ resume

A. employer asks you to fill in this form when you apply for a job

B. you make it up ahead of time, type it, send it in or take it with you

◆

C Words on Application Forms

When you apply for a job you often have to fill out an application form. The form may have a lot of special words on it. For example, it may ask for your **work experience, marital status,** number of **dependents,** and **references.**

work experience. Where you worked before. List of jobs you have had. All application forms ask about work experience.

marital status. Whether or not you are married. In some states, application forms are not supposed to ask about such private matters as marital status and number of dependents (see below).

dependents. People who depend on you for a living.

references. People who know you well and can tell what kind of person you are. Employers often ask for references before they hire someone. They may ask for "work references" (former bosses who can report on what kind of worker you were). Or they may ask for "personal references" (such people as teachers or ministers or friends of the family — but not members of your immediate family — who know you well enough to say what kind of person you are).

Questions

1. Sal Marino's wife stays home to take care of their two young children. Sal also has an older daughter who has her own apartment and supports herself.

   How many dependents does Sal have? ____

2. Which of these people would be good to use for personal references? (Check one or more.)

   __ **A.** your father

   __ **B.** your high school math teacher, who thinks you were a very good student

   __ **C.** your mother's boss, who has known you since you were a baby

3. What is Sal Marino's marital status? (See question 1.)

   __ **A.** single

   __ **B.** married

   __ **C.** divorced

All application forms ask about your *job history*. They will want you to list your *former jobs*, with a short description of each job and the dates when you had it. Usually they ask you to list your *current job* first. Or, if you are not working now, they will ask you to list your *last job* first, and then your *previous jobs.*

> **job history** (or *employment history*). List of jobs you have had. Same as work experience.

> **current job — former jobs.** Your *current* job is the job you have now. Your *former jobs* are the jobs you used to have.

> **last job — previous jobs.** Your *last job* is the most recent job you have had. Your *previous jobs* were the jobs you had before that.

Questions

1. Match.

__ where you work now   **A.** current job

__ where you worked before   **B.** former job

2. *Former job* means almost the same as —

__ **A.** current job

__ **B.** previous job

3. *Last job* means —

__ **A.** first job you ever had

__ **B.** job you just left

4. Marital status.

__ **A.** how many children you have

__ **B.** name of your husband or wife

__ **C.** whether or not you are married

5. References (in a job application form).

__ **A.** people who know you well

__ **B.** things you like

__ **C.** where you got your facts

◆

The application form may ask you to list the *immediate supervisor* you had on each job. It may ask you to list your *job title* and your reason for leaving. It may ask the *termination* date of the job. Some forms ask whether or not you were *terminated.*

> **immediate supervisor.** A *supervisor* is a boss. Your *immediate supervisor* is the boss directly above you.

> **job title.** What the job is called.

> **termination — terminated.** The *termination* of a job is simply the date you left. But to be *terminated* from a job means to be fired.

Questions

1. Anne Brown works as a supervisor in the billing department in the ABC Company.

   What's Anne's job title?

   __ **A.** billing department

   __ **B.** supervisor in billing department

   __ **C.** works for ABC Company

2. The head of the billing department where Anne works is Leona Smith. The president of the company is Ginger Adams.

   Who is Anne's immediate supervisor?

   __ **A.** Leona Smith

   __ **B.** Ginger Adams

3. Mark didn't show up for work on Tuesday and was told he had lost his job.

   Was he terminated?

   __ yes   __ no

◆

The application form will also ask about your schooling. It will probably ask you to list references.

Some forms also ask all sorts of special questions about you. For example:

- What is your *citizenship?*
- Have you ever been *bonded?*
- Have you ever been *convicted of a felony?*
- Are you *bondable?*

Then, after certain of these questions, the form may ask you to *specify.* (Note again that in some states, application forms are not supposed to ask about some of these personal matters, such as citizenship.)

citizenship. Country which you are legally part of. Your legal nationality. Most people are citizens of the countries where they were born.

bonded. A special kind of insurance to protect the company in case the employee steals from it. People who work with a lot of money on the job are often bonded. This means that if they steal money, the company will get the money back from the insurance company.

convicted of a felony. To be *convicted* means to be found guilty by a court of law. To be convicted of a *felony* means to be found guilty of a *serious crime.*

bondable. Means your record for honesty is good enough so the insurance company will bond you. If you've been convicted of a felony, you may not be bondable.

specify. Give details.

Questions

1. John Andrews stole $30,000 from the XYZ Company. John was bonded. He was caught and went to jail.

   The insurance company paid $30,000 to —

   __ **A.** John

   __ **B.** the XYZ Company

2. Has John ever been convicted of a felony?

   __ yes   __ no

3. Do you think John is bondable?

   __ yes   __ no

4. Specify the reasons for your answer to Question 3.

   _____

   _____

5. *Specify* means —

   __ **A.** be exact

   __ **B.** don't say too much

   __ **C.** forget it

Chapter Review

1. Match.

__ company you work for   **A.** dependent
__ job holder   **B.** employee
__ person who wants a job   **C.** employer
__ person you support   **D.** job applicant

2. Match.

__ immediate supervisor
__ job title
__ reference

A. your minister, one of your teachers, or another person who knows you well
B. the boss right above you
C. what the job is called

3. Match.

__ charges fee
__ found in big companies
__ government insurance program
__ may run summer youth program

A. JTPA
B. personnel office
C. private employment agency
D. Social Security

4. Match.

__ for people under 16
__ in newspapers
__ typed summary of jobs and schooling
__ goes with resume

A. classified ads
B. resume
C. cover letter
D. work permit

5. Match.

__ most recent job   **A.** former job
__ job before that   **B.** last job

6. Match.

__ part of government, gets people jobs
__ serious crime
__ your country

A. citizenship
B. felony
C. SES

7. Match.

__ listing
__ marital status
__ Social Security number

A. Are you married?
B. opening
C. you always keep the same one

8. Match.

__ fired
__ if you steal on the job, the company is insured

A. bonded
B. terminated

9. Match.

__ details
__ end
__ good risk

A. bondable
B. specify
C. termination

2
KINDS OF JOBS, TYPES OF BUSINESSES

Words in this chapter:

full-time job — part-time job
temporary job — permanent job
unskilled job
semi-skilled job
skilled job
clerical job
trainee
white collar job
blue collar job
self-employed
free-lance work
Civil Service job
manufacturer

jobber
distributor
wholesaler
retail
wholesale
importer
exporter
outlet
chain store
discount chain
franchise store
service business
agency
professional business

A What Kind of Job?

Have you decided what kind of job you want? Do you want a *full-time job,* or a *part-time job?* Do you want a *temporary job* or a *permanent job?*

full-time job — part-time job. On a *full-time job* you usually work 35 to 40 hours per week. On a *part-time job* you may only work a few hours per day. Or perhaps just on weekends. Or just in the evening.

temporary job — permanent job. A *temporary job* only lasts for a certain amount of time. (Like a summer job, or a job that only lasts a few weeks.) A *permanent job* is a regular job, a job that is expected to last a long time.

Questions

1. Marco works 8 hours on Saturday and 4 hours on Sunday. During the week he goes to school.

   __ **A.** full-time job
   __ **B.** part-time job

2. Marco has had this job (in Question 1) for 3 years. His boss will keep him as long as he wants the job.

   __ **A.** permanent part-time job
   __ **B.** temporary full-time job

3. Match.

   __ for 3 weeks at Christmas time

   __ from 7 in the morning until 3 in the afternoon, 5 days a week

   __ 3 nights per week

   A. full-time
   B. part-time
   C. temporary

In your first job, you are likely to start off with an *unskilled* job. Or in a simple *clerical* job. Or as a *trainee.* It usually takes time and training to get a *semi-skilled* job or *skilled* job.

unskilled — semi-skilled — skilled. An *unskilled* job is a job where you don't need any special skills. A *semi-skilled* job requires a certain amount of skills and training. A *skilled* job requires a lot of skills. A carpenter's job or a plumber's job is a skilled job. Some machines can be run by semi-skilled workers. But if the machine is very tough it requires a skilled worker.

clerical job. The job of a clerk. Very simple clerical jobs do not require any special skills. Higher level clerical jobs may require typing and other office skills.

trainee. A beginning worker who is being trained to handle a job.

Questions

1. Match.

___ electrician   **A.** skilled job

___ laborer   **B.** trainee

___ person learning the   **C.** unskilled job
     job of electrician

2. Beginning clerk.

___ **A.** skilled

___ **B.** unskilled

3. "Semi-," as in "semi-skilled."

___ **A.** not at all

___ **B.** partly

___ **C.** very

Today there are more **white collar** jobs than **blue collar** jobs.

> **white collar job.** A job in an office. Or any other job where you don't do much physical work.

> **blue collar job.** A laboring job. A job in a factory. Or in construction. Or any other type of job where you do a lot of physical work.

Questions

1. Works for a bank.

___ **A.** blue collar

___ **B.** white collar

2. Sales job.

___ **A.** blue collar

___ **B.** white collar

3. Clerk in an office.

___ **A.** blue collar

___ **B.** white collar

4. Laborer, building roads.

___ **A.** blue collar

___ **B.** white collar

Not all people get jobs as employees of businesses. Some people are **self-employed**. Some people do **free-lance** work. Some people have **Civil Service** jobs.

self-employed. Work for yourself. Have your own small business. Or do **free-lance** work (see below).

free-lance work. When you do free-lance work you work on your own and do special jobs for other people. You get paid by the job.

Civil Service jobs. Jobs in government. You usually have to pass a test to get a Civil Service job.

Questions

1. Free-lance artist.

__ **A.** gets paid by the job
__ **B.** works for a salary

2. Match.

__ does typing jobs at home
__ Washington, D.C., policeman

A. Civil Service job
B. free-lance job

B Types of Business

There are many types of business to work for. For example, you might get a job with a **manufacturer.** Or you might get a job with a **jobber** or **distributor.** Or you might get a job with a **retailer.**

manufacturer. Factory. A manufacturer makes things to be sold.

jobber or **distributor** or **wholesaler.** Sells things to other businesses for them to sell to the public. A jobber or distributor usually buys from manufacturers and sells to *retail businesses* (see below).

retail business. A business that buys things from manufacturers or wholesalers and sells to the public. The store you buy in are retail businesses.

Questions

1. Many **manufacturers** sell things to **wholesalers** who then sell to **retailers.**

   Who would you expect to sell at the **lowest** prices?

   __ **A.** manufacturer
   __ **B.** wholesaler
   __ **C.** retailer

2. Which would you expect to sell at the **highest** prices?

   __ **A.** manufacturer
   __ **B.** wholesaler
   __ **C.** retailer

3. What kind of business is the local food store where you shop?

   __ **A.** retail
   __ **B.** wholesale

4. **Jobber**, compared to manufacturer and retail.

   __ **A.** beginning
   __ **B.** middle
   __ **C.** end

◆

A manufacturer or distributor sells goods **wholesale** to other businesses. The other businesses sell at **retail.**

wholesale. When a business sells wholesale it usually sells to other businesses in big quantities at low prices.

retail. Then the other businesses sell to customers at "retail" prices, one at a time, at higher prices, and still make money.

Businesses that sell wholesale are sometimes called "wholesalers," while businesses that sell retail are sometimes called "retailers."

Questions

1. The XYZ Company sells the Hobby World Shop its games for $5.00. The Hobby World Shop sells the games for $9.95.

   Match.

   ___ $5.00   **A.** retail

   ___ $9.95   **B.** wholesale

2. A jobber is —

   ___ **A.** a retailer

   ___ **B.** a wholesaler

Some of the things we buy are made in other countries. And some of the things we manufacture are sold in other countries. The businesses which specialize in trade with foreign countries are called *importers* and *exporters.*

> **importer.** Buys things from other countries to sell here.

> **exporter.** Sells U.S. goods to foreign countries.

Questions

1. Goldberg and Sons buys radios from Japan for sale in the U.S.

   ___ **A.** importer

   ___ **B.** exporter

2. BQR Sales specializes in selling wheat to other countries.

   ___ **A.** importer

   ___ **B.** exporter

Let's take a look at different types of retail *outlets.* Some of the most common types are *chain stores.* Some of these chain stores are *discount chain stores.* Some of the chains set up *franchise stores.*

> **outlet.** A place that sells things. A retail outlet is a business that sells to the public.

> **chain store.** A part of a "chain." That is, part of a whole group of stores run by one company. Usually the stores have the same name and the same policies.

> **discount chain.** A chain of stores that claims to sell things at a "discount," that is, at lower prices.

> **franchise store.** Some big retail firms sell franchises. The people who buy a franchise set up a store that uses the name of the big firm and sells its goods. A franchise store is pretty much the same as any other chain store, except it has separate owners.

Questions

1. The word "outlet" can mean many things. One meaning is the place where you plug in an electric cord. Outlet can also mean a store.

   In this book, outlet means —

   __ **A.** place to plug in electric cord
   __ **B.** store

2. Samantha owns the local doughnut store. It's one of the Donut King Stores, which you see in many places. She had to pay Donut King money to use its name. It sold her the equipment for the store. It delivers supplies every day, which it sells to Samantha.

   Is her store a franchise store?

   __ yes   __ no

3. You probably have chain stores in your area.

   Do you have a K-Mart?

   __ yes   __ no

   Do you have a J.C. Penneys?

   __ yes   __ no

   Name one other chain store.

   _____

4. Which of these is likely to be a chain store?

   __ **A.** distributor
   __ **B.** exporter
   __ **C.** supermarket

5. A particular type of T-shirt usually sells for $8.95 for a package of 3. One store in our neighborhood sells this package for $5.95.

   Match.

   __ $8.95   **A.** discount price
   __ $5.95   **B.** regular retail price

23

Not all businesses sell goods. Some businesses are *service businesses.* An *agency* is a service business. So is a *professional* business.

service business. Sells services instead of things. The service might be a ride in a cab. Or being taught something. Or having your car washed. Or having a letter typed for you.

agency. A type of service business. A travel agency helps you plan a trip. A model agency helps models get work. An employment agency helps people get jobs.

professional business. A business that sells the services of people with special training. Firms of lawyers, doctors, and accountants are all professional businesses.

Questions

1. Which of the following are service businesses? (Check one or more.)

___ **A.** airline

___ **B.** cuts hair

___ **C.** makes paper

___ **D.** rents cars

___ **E.** sells cars

2. Look back over the definition of agency. It tells about 3 different kinds of agency. The word "agency" appears in all 3 descriptions.

   What other word appears in all 3?

   h__ __ __ __

3. Do you think a dentist is a professional?

___ yes ___ no

4. Which of these people works in a professional business?

___ **A.** clerk in travel agency

___ **B.** nurse in doctor's office

Chapter Review

1. Match.

___ carpenter   **A.** unskilled

___ laborer   **B.** semi-skilled

___ machine operator, where the job takes 3 months to learn   **C.** skilled

2. Match.

___ office job   **A.** blue collar

___ factory job   **B.** white collar

3. Match.

___ distributor   **A.** jobber

___ makes the product   **B.** manufac-turer

___ sells to public   **C.** retailer

4. Match.

___ what the jobber gets from stores   **A.** retail price

___ what the stores charge   **B.** wholesale price

5. Match.

___ buys from foreign countries   **A.** exporter

___ sells to foreign countries   **B.** importer

6. Match.

___ job that only lasts a short time   **A.** full-time

___ job that lasts a long time   **B.** part-time

___ usually 35 or 40 hours per week   **C.** permanent

___ evenings or weekends   **D.** temporary

7. Match.

___ claims to sell at lower prices   **A.** agency

___ doctors' office   **B.** discount chain

___ helps you get travel tickets   **C.** profes-sional business

8. Match.

___ store   **A.** chain

___ whole group of stores   **B.** franchise

___ you can own it, but you have to pay to use the name   **C.** outlet

9. Match.

___ barber   **A.** often part of a chain

___ supermarket   **B.** service business

10. Match.

___ general office work   **A.** clerk

___ learning the job   **B.** trainee

___ working on your own   **C.** self-employed

11. Match.

___ paid by the job   **A.** free lance

___ work for the government   **B.** Civil Service

3
OFFICE WORKERS, SALESPEOPLE, AND COMPUTER JOBS

Words in this chapter:

secretary
clerk
bookkeeper
receptionist
switchboard operator
lite steno
executive secretary
shorthand
report to
gal/guy Friday
A/A
temp
office temp
accounts receivable (A/R)
accounts payable (A/P)
customer service
commission
salary plus commission

draw against commission
on the road
expense account
territory
sales rep
manufacturer's rep
to the trade
commission rep
data entry
CRT operator
keyboard
keypunch operator
data processing
word processing
computer operator
computer program
computer programmer

A Office Jobs

What kinds of jobs are there in offices? There are **secretaries,** of course. And many kinds of **clerks.** There are **bookkeepers.** In some offices there are **receptionists** and **switchboard operators.** These are just a few of the many kinds of jobs.

secretary. Handles paperwork for a boss. Types letters. Takes care of details. May answer phones.

clerk. General office work. A clerk does filing, works with the mail, may answer phones.

bookkeeper. Keeps money records. In addition to writing up the "books" (money records), a bookkeeper may keep track of money owed, write out checks, and so on. (Notice that "bookkeeper" is spelled with two o's, two k's, and two e's — right in a row.)

receptionist. Greets visitors to the office. Usually also answers phones. The same person may be both receptionist and **switchboard operator** (see below).

switchboard operator. In the place where you work there may be a lot of telephones. If your company has a switchboard operator, the operator answers calls and puts them through to the right people. The switchboard operator may also be asked to dial long distance calls for people in the office. When not busy, a switchboard operator may be asked to do some light typing or simple clerical work.

Questions

1. In which of these types of jobs do employees sometimes answer phones? (Choose one or more.)

___ **A.** clerk

___ **B.** receptionist

___ **C.** secretary

___ **D.** switchboard operator

2. Match each quality with the type of job where it is **most** important. (But note that all of these qualities are good for office jobs.)

___ good at numbers   **A.** bookkeeper

___ good voice on the phone **B.** receptionist

___ warm and friendly with   **C.** switchboard
people you meet in   operator
person

3. Office clerk.

___ **A.** blue collar

___ **B.** white collar

4. Who do you think is likely to be more skilled?

___ **A.** beginning clerk

___ **B.** beginning secretary

5. Match.

___ does work for the   **A.** secretary
whole office   **B.** switchboard
___ works directly for a boss   operator

27

A beginning secretary has to be able to type and usually to take at least *lite steno.*

An *executive secretary* will probably need all sorts of skills, including fast *shorthand.*

lite steno. "Steno" is short for stenography. Stenography is a code for writing down very fast what someone dictates to you. A secretary who only takes "lite steno" is not very skilled at it and is only expected to take a small amount of dictation.

executive secretary. Highly skilled secretary who works under a high-level boss.

shorthand. Same as stenography.

Questions

1. Match.

__ beginning secretary

__ executive secretary

A. likely to work for low-level boss

B. likely to work for president of company

2. What is the advantage of steno?

__ **A.** big

__ **B.** fast

__ **C.** pretty

3. Ms. Jacobi is a sales manager. Every morning she dictates between 10 and 20 letters. Once a week she dictates a sales memo. Some of these sales memos are 15 to 20 pages long.

Would you call this lite steno?

__ yes __ no

4. Why do you think steno is sometimes called shorthand?

__ **A.** for people with short fingers

__ **B.** short way of writing

When you go to work in an office, your boss may be the office manager. Or you may *report* directly to one of the other bosses. For example, you may have a job as a *"gal/guy Friday,"* or as an *A/A.*

report to. Work for. Take directions from (a boss).

gal/guy Friday. Assistant to a boss. A "gal" or "guy Friday" may not have the skills of a secretary, but is expected to help out in whatever office work has to be done. ("Friday" was a character in the story *Robinson Crusoe,* who helped Crusoe stay alive when his ship was wrecked and he was stranded on an island.)

A/A. Stands for **A**dministrative **A**ssistant. An A/A is pretty much the same as a gal/guy Friday, helping out in an office in whatever has to be done. But in some offices, a person with the job title of administrative assistant has a lot of experience and is given a lot of responsibility.

Questions

1. "Friday" in "gal/guy Friday."

   __ **A.** day of week

   __ **B.** person in book

2. When you report to someone, you —

   __ **A.** give orders

   __ **B.** take orders

3. What do an A/A and a gal/guy Friday have in common?

   __ **A.** help out in a little bit of everything

   __ **B.** only work at very special things

4. When you "administer" you manage things. When you "assist" you help.

   Match.

   __ first A in A/A   **A.** helper

   __ second A in A/A   **B.** running things

◆

The ads for office jobs sometimes talk about *"temps,"* or *"office temps."* Do you know what these words mean?

> **temp.** A temporary job. A job that only lasts a short time.

> **office temp.** A temporary job in an office.

Questions

1. Harry gets jobs through the XYZ Employment Agency. He calls up in the morning to see what jobs there are that day. He goes to a different office almost every day he works. Sometimes he does filing. Sometimes he answers phones. Sometimes he does bookkeeping.

   Do you think Harry is an office temp?

   __ yes   __ no

2. Temp.

   __ **A.** short for temperature

   __ **B.** short for temporary

◆

Some of the jobs in a big office might be in *accounts receivable.* Others might be in *accounts payable.* Still others might be in *customer service.*

> **accounts receivable.** The part of the business that deals with customers ("accounts") who have bought goods and owe the company money. The people in accounts receivable do billing. They keep track of how much money is owed, when it is due to be paid, and so on. And each month they may send customers "statements," to let them know what they still owe and what they paid that month. Sometimes called A/R for short.

accounts payable. The part of the business that deals with keeping track of whom (the "accounts") the company owes money to and how much. The people in accounts payable pay the bills. Sometimes called A/P for short.

customer service. The part of the company that handles customer complaints and problems.

Questions

1. Merrilee is taking care of a customer who complains an order wasn't shipped when it was promised.

__ **A.** accounts receivable

__ **B.** accounts payable

__ **C.** customer service

2. Where is a bookkeeper most likely to work?

__ **A.** accounts payable

__ **B.** customer service

3. Match.

__ company bought a computer and still owes money for it

__ customer bought a refrigerator and still owes money for it

__ warehouse sent the order to the wrong customer

A. accounts receivable

B. accounts payable

C. customer service

Review

1. Match.

__ A/A   **A.** helps out in running an office

__ steno   **B.** job that only lasts a short time

__ temp   **C.** shorthand

2. Which job requires the best skills?

__ **A.** executive secretary

__ **B.** gal/guy Friday

__ **C.** office temp

3. Match.

__ report to

__ take shorthand

__ work in customer service

A. handle problems

B. work for

C. write down what someone dictates

4. Gal/guy Friday.

__ **A.** boss

__ **B.** helper

5. Accounts receivable.

__ **A.** pay bills

__ **B.** send bills to customers

B Jobs in Selling

Some salespersons work on straight *commission.* Others get a salary with no commission, or a *salary plus commission.* Others work on a *draw against commission.*

commission. Amount of pay based on how much is sold. The usual commission is a percent of sales. If the commission is supposed to be 10% and the sale is $100, the salesperson earns $10.

salary plus commission. A fixed salary plus a percent of what the salesperson sells. Let's say the salesperson earns $150 per week plus 5% of sales. In one week total sales were $500. The total pay was $150 (salary) plus $25 commission (5% times $500), which added together equals $175.

draw against commission. An arrangement where a salesperson works on commission but makes a fixed amount (the "draw") even if commissions for that period didn't equal that much. Example: Let's say you have a draw of $200 per week against a 10% commission. You have to sell a total of $2,000 to equal your draw (10% times $2,000 equal $200). If your sales are more than $2,000 you earn more than $200 — whatever the commission comes out to. If your sales are less than $2,000 you still get the $200 draw.

Questions

1. Enrico earns 5% of anything he sells. He is guaranteed $1,000 per month even if he doesn't earn that much.

   Match.

   __ 5%   **A.** commission
   __ $1,000 per month   **B.** draw

2. Lucia is paid $160 a week salary in her sales job plus 2% of her sales. Her total sales for the week were $1,600, and 2% of this is $32.

   How much did Lucia earn in total?

   $_____

3. Joshua is starting a new sales job. He can either have a straight salary or a salary plus commission. Which choice will give him a chance to earn more if he sells a lot?

   __ **A.** straight salary
   __ **B.** salary plus commission

4. Penelope is also a salesperson. She earns $165 per week. She doesn't earn anything on top of this as a percentage of sales.

   Match.

   __ Enrico (Question 1)   **A.** straight salary
   __ Lucia (Question 2)   **B.** salary plus commission
   __ Penelope   **C.** draw against commission

5. The salary part of Joshua's income (Question 3 above) will probably be higher if he chooses —

   __ **A.** straight salary
   __ **B.** salary plus commission

A salesperson *on the road* usually has an *expense account.* A salesperson on the road sometimes has a large *territory* to cover.

on the road. A salesperson on the road goes from city to city.

expense account. Money a salesperson gets back for the costs of travel and entertaining customers. For example, your company may give you a certain amount for any day you're on the road, or a certain amount for the miles you travel, or up to a certain amount for your hotels and meals, or repayment for anything you spend on meals for customers, or repayment for phone calls, tolls, postage, and so on. Some companies give cars to their salespeople. Other companies pay you a certain amount each month to use your own car. The expense account a company allows its salespeople is usually a combination of the things above.

territory. The area a salesperson sells in.

Questions

1. Maureen gets $500 per month plus 7½ percent of anything she sells plus $250 per month to pay the costs of running the car she uses on the job.

   Match.

   __ $500 per month   **A.** commission

   __ 7½ percent   **B.** expense account

   __ $250 per month   **C.** salary

2. The home office of the firm Maureen works for is in Dallas. But she is hardly ever there because her job is to sell to her customers in Georgia.

   What is her territory?

   __ **A.** Dallas

   __ **B.** Georgia

3. In a typical week, Maureen spends one day per week in her office in Atlanta and 4 days traveling around Georgia.

   She spends most of her selling time on the road.

   __ True   __ False

Some *sales reps* are *manufacturer's reps* who only *sell to the trade.* They may work on a straight salary, or they may be *commission reps.*

sales rep. Short for sales representative, or salesperson. To "rep" a line of products means to represent it, that is, to sell it. The rep may be an employee of the company whose goods he or she sells. Or he or she may be an independent business person.

manufacturer's rep. A salesperson who works for a manufacturer.

to the trade. To sell wholesale. The "trade" are the companies that specialize in a special type of product. When you sell only to the trade you sell only to other companies which may in turn sell to the public.

commission rep. A salesperson who works on commission.

Questions

1. Olga is a saleswoman for Purity Plastics, which makes plastic slip covers for chairs and sofas. She only sells to stores. She makes a straight salary.

   Is she a commission rep?

   __ yes   __ no

2. Is she a manufacturer's rep?

   __ yes   __ no

3. Does she sell to the trade?

   __ yes   __ no

4. "Rep" is short for "representative" the same as "steno" is short for stenography.

   Match.

   __ rep   **A.** steno
   __ representative   **B.** stenography

5. Which is a salesperson to the trade?

   __ **A.** sells tires to auto stores
   __ **B.** sells tires retail

Review

1. Match.

   __ commission   **A.** guarantee
   __ draw   **B.** pay for travel
   __ expense account **C.** percent of sales

2. Territory.

   __ **A.** things you sell
   __ **B.** where you sell

3. To the trade.

   __ **A.** retail
   __ **B.** wholesale

4. Rep.

   __ **A.** pay back
   __ **B.** sell

5. Salespersons on the road are traveling salespersons.

   __ True   __ False

33

C Computer Jobs

In most present-day computers, **data entry** is done by a **CRT operator** working on a **keyboard.** In some of the older computers, data entry is done by a **keypunch operator.**

data entry. The job of putting information ("data") into a computer. For example, a store that uses a computer to make up bills for customers needs someone to type into the computer the customers' names, addresses, what they bought, how much they owe, and so on. This is the data. The computer can use the data to make up the customers' bills and can keep track of the data in its "memory."

CRT operator. Someone with the job of data entry. CRT stands for **C**athode **R**ay **T**ube. This is the TV screen that is part of modern computer systems. The CRT operator types the data in. This information shows up on the CRT and goes into the computer's memory at the same time.

keyboard. What the CRT operator types on. A computer keyboard looks like a typewriter. The letters and numbers are arranged pretty much the same way as on a typewriter.

keypunch operator. A person who feeds information into certain older types of computers. In these older computers, information is typed on a machine that punches holes in cards, and the pattern of holes gives the information to the computer.

Questions

1. Sam's company uses its computer to make out paychecks for its employees. One of Sam's jobs is to type in how many hours each employee worked.

   Is that data entry?

   __ yes   __ no

2. A CRT operator's job is sort of like the job of —

   __ **A.** boss

   __ **B.** receptionist

   __ **C.** salesperson

   __ **D.** typist

3. Match.

   __ holes in cards   **A.** CRT operator

   __ TV screen   **B.** keypunch operator

4. "Keyboard," as used above.

   __ like a piano

   __ like a typewriter

5. Match.

   __ new   **A.** CRT systems

   __ old   **B.** keypunch systems

34

Businesses use computers for *data processing*. They also use computers for *word processing*.

data processing. Use of a computer to enter and organize information. For example, a computer that prepares paychecks can do the arithmetic to figure out the number of hours worked times the pay per hour, subtract taxes, and so on — and then print out the paychecks.

word processing. The use of a computer to write and type letters, memos, even books. The word processing computer stores what you've typed on it. You can change a letter, a word, or a line at a time. You can also give it directions to tell it how to line things up, how big the type should be, and so on. When you are all finished you can have it type out automatically the finished letter or memo. And if you want you can have it type out several copies.

Questions

1. Match.

__ enter and organize **A.** data

__ information **B.** processing

2. Word processing might be used to —

__ **A.** do billing and bookkeeping

__ **B.** get a newspaper ready to print

A *computer operator* knows how to use a *computer program* but doesn't write them. That's the job of a *computer programmer*.

computer operator. Runs the computer. In a small computer set-up, the same person may both do data entry and be the computer operator. But where there are separate CRT operators and a computer operator, the CRT operators simply type in information. The computer operator does all the special tasks to get the computer to do the correct job of data processing.

computer program. Set of directions that tells a computer how to do a particular task. These directions are typed into the computer in one of the special coded computer "languages." (There are many of these languages.)

computer programmer. A person who is skilled at understanding a computer language and can use this language to write computer programs.

Questions

1. Which job is likely to require the most training?

__ **A.** CRT operator

__ **B.** computer operator

__ **C.** computer programmer

2. Match.

__ types in information about a person's bill   **A.** CRT operator

__ writes a program to have the computer do billing   **B.** computer operator

__ uses the program to have the computer print out the billing information   **C.** computer programmer

3. Which is most like solving a problem?

__ **A.** entering data

__ **B.** following a program's instructions

__ **C.** writing a program

Chapter Review

1. Match.

__ to "rep," as a salesperson

__ to work for

  A. report to

  B. represent

2. Match.

__ named for a helpful character in a book

__ only has to have lite steno

__ very highly skilled

  A. gal/guy Friday

  B. beginning secretary

  C. executive secretary

3. Match.

__ job that only lasts a short time

__ similar to gal/guy Friday

__ same as stenography

  A. A/A

  B. office temp

  C. shorthand

4. Match.

__ doing billing

__ handling complaints

__ paying bills

  A. accounts payable

  B. accounts receivable

  C. customer service

5. Match.

__ gets paid for travel and entertainment costs

__ gets 10% of sales

__ gets 10% of sales *and* is guaranteed $750 per month

__ gets $140 per week plus 2% of sales

  A. draw against commission

  B. expense account

  C. salary plus commission

  D. straight commission

6. Match.

__ sales area

__ to the trade

__ traveling

  A. manufacturer's rep

  B. on the road

  C. territory

7. Match.

__ general office work

__ greeting, in person

__ money records

__ phones

  A. bookkeeper

  B. clerk

  C. receptionist

  D. switchboard operator

8. Match.

__ does data entry

__ runs computer

__ skilled at using special computer language to give instructions to computer

  A. CRT operator

  B. computer operator

  C. computer programmer

9. Match.

__ for writing and typing letters

__ putting in information

__ organization of information

__ set of instructions to tell computer what to do

  A. data entry

  B. data processing

  C. program

  D. word processing

10. Match.

__ CRT

__ keypunch

__ keyboard

  A. like a typewriter

  B. puts holes in cards

  C. TV screen

4
MANUFACTURING AND CONSTRUCTION

Words in this chapter:

plant
assembly line
machine operator
assembler
packer
apprentice
shop foreman
supervisor
conveyor belt
dolly
hand truck
skid
pallet
fork lift
maintenance
jam
machine adjuster
down time
quality control
machinist
blueprints
job specifications (or "specs")
to machine
close tolerance
robotics
mason

welder
electrician
crane operator
licensed
contractor
journeyman
builder
developer
light construction
heavy construction
building renovation
road construction
demolition
grading
site
foundation
to frame a house
studs
plumbing lines
electrical conduit
sheetrock
plasterboard
drywall construction
prefab
modular

A Manufacturing

Let's say you want to get a starting job in a manufacturing *plant.* What kind of job will you get?

You may work on an *assembly line.* Perhaps you will be trained to be a *machine operator.* Or maybe you will get a job as an *assembler.* Or perhaps as a *packer.*

plant. Factory.

assembly line. In some factories, the product being made is moved along a line from one person to another and from one machine to another while it is being manufactured. If you have a job in an assembly line, you do one of the different jobs in this process.

machine operator. Person who runs a machine.

assembler. A worker in a factory who puts together different parts of a product.

packer. A worker who packs the product, to get it ready for shipment.

Questions

1. Person in an assembly line.

__ **A.** does all the job
__ **B.** does only one job

2. Manufacturing plant.

__ **A.** grows things
__ **B.** makes things

3. A particular toy has 6 different parts. Someone has to put the 6 parts together. Then another person puts the finished toy into a box, puts tape around the box, and puts it into a stack, ready for shipment.

Match.

__ first person   **A.** assembler
__ second person   **B.** packer

4. Do you think you might find machine operators in some assembly lines?

__ yes   __ no

---◆---

Your first job in an industrial plant may be as an *apprentice* or trainee. You can't expect to be a *shop foreman* or *supervisor* right from the beginning.

apprentice. A beginning worker who works under the direction of a skilled worker to learn a skilled job.

shop foreman. A worker who is in charge of a group of other workers.

supervisor. A boss. A shop foreman is a supervisor. He or she is the boss of a small group of workers. His or her boss may run a whole department. The boss running the department is also a supervisor.

Questions

1. Match.

___ gives orders   **A.** apprentice

___ takes orders   **B.** foreman

2. Match.

___ gives orders   **A.** apprentice

___ learning job   **B.** supervisor

How do you move goods from one place to another in a factory? One way is on a ***conveyor belt.*** Another way is on a ***dolly*** or ***hand truck.***

> **conveyor belt.** A wide belt on metal rollers that goes from one location to another in a factory. A machine keeps the belt moving. Objects on the belt are carried with it as it moves.
>
> **dolly.** A low platform on wheels. You put things on the dolly and push or pull it.
>
> **hand truck.** A device for moving heavy objects or a stack of boxes. You stack the objects on a small metal platform on the ground with 2 wheels in the back. The hand truck is pushed like a wheelbarrow.

Questions

1. Match.

A. dolly

B. hand truck

2. Match.

___ move a conveyor belt   **A.** pull

___ move a dolly   **B.** turn on machine

3. Match.

___ moving belt   **A.** conveyor

___ platform on 4 wheels   **B.** dolly

___ 2 wheels, metal platform   **C.** hand truck

If the goods are on *skids,* or *pallets,* you can use a *fork lift* to move them.

skid. A wooden platform built to stand a few inches off the ground. You stack boxes or put other goods on the skid to keep them off the ground. This keeps them dry if there is a flood. It also makes it easy for a *fork lift* to move them (see below).

pallet. Same as skid.

fork lift. A machine with metal "forks" on the bottom which can be pushed under a skid and then raised. With the load raised up it can be moved from place to place. Some fork lifts are run by gas engines. They look sort of like trucks. Others are run by electricity.

Questions

1. Match.

__ fork lift

__ pallet

A.

B.

2. Which has wheels?

__ **A.** dolly

__ **B.** skid

3. Match.

__ move a dolly   **A.** pull

__ move a pallet   **B.** use a fork lift

4. Match.

__ push   **A.** fork lift

__ often has gas engine   **B.** hand truck

◆

Maintenance is an important part of any industry. All machines *jam* or break down from time to time. Maintenance workers and *machine adjusters* try to prevent *down time* and maintain good *quality control.*

maintenance. Keeping machines in good working order.

jam. A machine jam is just what it sounds like. Things get stuck in the machine and it stops.

machine adjuster. Some machines have to be adjusted frequently, either to make sure they keep running OK or to "set them up" for a new job. Some plants have separate machine adjusters to do this job. A machine adjuster also does machine repairs and maintenance.

down time. The amount of time a machine is not working. A breakdown of a machine causes down time.

quality control. Making sure the products being made are of good quality.

Questions

1. Match.

__ good maintenance

__ poor maintenance

    A. results in lots of down time

    B. not so much down time

2. Does a jam cause down time?

__ yes   __ no

3. Match.

__ runs machines

__ fixes machines

    A. adjuster

    B. operator

4. You've probably bought many things in your life where the quality control was poor.

Describe one of these things.

_____

_____

Some machines can only be run by trained *machinists.* A machinist may have to work with *blueprints* or other *job specifications.*

machinist. A skilled machine operator. Or a person who makes machines and tools.

blueprints. Special drawings and plans to tell exactly how something is to be made. Blueprints are usually technical. You need to learn how to understand them.

job specifications (or "**specs**"). Any way of telling you how the job is to be done. For some job specifications you need blueprints. Other job "specs" are written out.

Questions

1. Specs, as used above.

__ **A.** eyeglasses

__ **B.** instructions

2. Are blueprints sometimes part of job specifications?

__ yes   __ no

3. Match.

__ adjuster

__ machinist

    A. fixer

    B. operator

4. Blueprints.

__ **A.** easy to understand

__ **B.** hard to understand

A machinist may have to *machine* products to *close tolerances.*

to machine. To make or shape something — usually metal — by cutting or grinding it in a machine.

close tolerances. The amount of tolerance you have on a job is the amount of difference you are allowed in the size of the thing you're making. If you are working with "close tolerances" you have to make sure the part is made almost exactly to the perfect size.

Questions

1. Close tolerances.

___ **A.** has to fit

___ **B.** lots of leeway

2. To machine, as used here.

___ **A.** cut or shape

___ **B.** turn on

Have you ever heard the word "*robotics*"? Do you know what it means?

robotics. The science of using "robots" to do jobs humans have always had to do. Robots are being used more and more in industrial jobs. You probably remember the robots in the old movies. They were machines that were made to look like humans. The modern ones don't look like that. But they can do tougher and tougher jobs.

Questions

1. Robotics refers to —

___ **A.** toys

___ **B.** complex machines

2. How are the modern robots used in factories similar to humans?

___ **A.** they do the same jobs

___ **B.** they look the same

Review

1. Match.

___ wooden platform   **A.** dolly

___ wooden platform on   **B.** skid
    wheels

2. Match.

___ fork lift   **A.** lifts up
    pallets
___ hand truck
    B. push it
    like a wheel-
    barrow

3. Match.

___ jam   **A.** how much
    leeway you
___ tolerance   have

    B. makes
    machines
    stop

4. Shop foreman.

___ **A.** learning the job

___ **B.** one of the bosses

5. Match.

___ blueprint   **A.** machine
    not running
___ down time
    B. tells you
___ robot   how to do the
    job

    C. type of
    machine

6. Match.

___ adjuster   **A.** fixes
    machines
___ apprentice
    B. learning
___ assembler   skilled job

    C. puts parts
    together

7. Good quality control.

___ **A.** to improve factories

___ **B.** to improve machines

___ **C.** to improve products

8. Manufacturing plant.

___ **A.** factory

___ **B.** machine

___ **C.** worker

B Construction

Masons, welders, electricians, crane operators, and other skilled workers make good money in construction jobs.

These jobs all take training and experience. In most cases, you have to be *licensed* to get a job like this.

mason. A worker who builds with stone or brick, or stone and concrete.

welder. A worker who uses a welding machine, with a very hot flame, to join metal pieces together.

electrician. You have probably had electricians come into your house to fix electrical things that are broken. Electricians on a construction job install the electrical system. They put in new wiring, cables, electrical fixtures, and so on.

crane operator. Cranes are the big machines you have seen that lift heavy loads at construction sites.

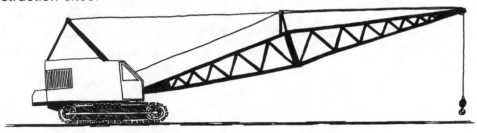

licensed. The skilled workers in construction are often licensed. To get a license they have to pass a test and have a certain amount of training and experience.

Questions

1. Match.

___ metal   **A.** electrician

___ stone   **B.** mason

___ wires   **C.** welder

2. There is a type of bird called a crane. The shape of its neck makes it look sort of like a construction crane.

What kind of neck do you think it has?

___ **A.** long

___ **B.** short

3. Licensed construction workers are —

___ **A.** skilled

___ **B.** unskilled

There are also plenty of unskilled jobs in construction. A job as an **apprentice,** or even as a laborer, working for a construction **contractor** can be a good job. And the job of apprentice can lead you to become a **journeyman.**

apprentice. You've seen this word before. An apprentice is a beginning worker who works under the direction of a skilled worker. To become a licensed mason or electrician you often have to spend several years as an apprentice.

contractor. A contractor is the company that is hired to do the construction job. A contractor on a large construction job may have several "subcontractors." For example, there may be a subcontractor just for doing the electricity, another one for doing the masonry, and so on.

journeyman. A skilled, professional worker, one who is no longer an apprentice.

Questions

1. Is a licensed carpenter a skilled worker?

__ yes   __ no

2. Is a journeyman plumber a skilled worker?

__ yes   __ no

3. Who is likely to get more pay?

__ **A.** apprentice

__ **B.** journeyman

4. Match.

__ responsible for whole job

__ only responsible for part of the job

A. contractor

B. subcontractor

You might get a job working for a **builder** or a **developer,** if there is a lot of construction work where you live.

builder. A person or business whose specialty is putting up buildings. Sometimes a builder puts up buildings for other people. Other times the builder holds on to the buildings with the idea of selling them later.

developer. A builder who builds large projects, such as shopping centers or whole neighborhoods with lots of houses. A developer handles the complex legal and money matters of the project as well as supervising the actual construction.

Questions

1. Can a builder be a contractor?

__ yes   __ no

2. Developer.

__ **A.** just finished a project with total of 200 houses

__ **B.** built 2 houses last year

3. Contractor.

__ **A.** builds for others

__ **B.** holds on to the buildings being built

Think of all the different kinds of construction there are. For example, *light construction.* *Heavy construction. Building renovation. Road construction.*

light construction. Small-scale building, where you don't need heavy machinery. Building houses is light construction.

heavy construction. Large-scale building, where you have to use heavy machinery. Roads, dams, bridges and skyscrapers are heavy construction.

building renovation. To remodel, or restore, an older building. To renovate a building, the contractor will often "gut" it, leaving just the bare walls, and then redo everything inside and out.

road construction. Building or repairing roads. Road construction is one of the main sources of construction jobs.

Questions

1. Building with 40 floors.

__ **A.** light construction

__ **B.** heavy construction

2. Adding a room to your house.

__ **A.** light construction

__ **B.** heavy construction

3. Bridge across the Mississippi River.

__ **A.** light construction

__ **B.** heavy construction

4. Road construction is considered heavy construction because it requires a lot of machines and heavy equipment.

__ True   __ False

5. Building renovation.

__ **A.** keep the old, make it look like new

__ **B.** tear it down and start all over

Building construction can mean more than actually putting up the building. It may begin with *demolition* of the old building. Then there is the job of *grading* the building *site* and laying the *foundation.*

demolition. Tearing down the old building.

grading. Smoothing out the land where the building is to be built.

site. The place where the building is to be set up.

foundation. The base of the building. The part under the ground. In a house, the basement is the foundation. In a skyscraper, there may be several floors underground.

Questions

1. Site, as used above.

__ **A.** piece of land

__ **B.** the way you see

2. Grading, as used above.

__ **A.** get the site ready

__ **B.** give grades

3. Match.

__ get rid of old house   **A.** demolition

__ rebuild old house   **B.** renovation

4. Which is part of the foundation?

__ **A.** basement

__ **B.** roof

__ **C.** windows

---◆---

To put up the walls of a house you *frame* it first. You may have to put in *studs* next. You want to put in *insulation.* You have to leave room for your *plumbing lines* and electrical *conduits.*

to frame a house. To put up the frame — the wood timbers that give shape and strength to the house, and that the walls are nailed to.

studs. The smaller upright timbers in a house. Inside walls are nailed to studs.

plumbing lines. The water pipes and the pipes that carry out waste material.

electrical conduit. A tube or "duct" that holds the electrical wires.

Questions

1. Plumbing lines.

__ **A.** carry water and waste

__ **B.** you draw them on a piece of paper

2. Studs.

__ **A.** made of gold

__ **B.** made of wood

3. Which comes first?

__ **A.** the frame

__ **B.** the conduits

4. Match.

__ conduit   **A.** electricity

__ frame   **B.** wood

◆

For the walls of a house, you will probably use **sheetrock,** or **plasterboard,** or some other kind of **drywall construction.**

> **sheetrock.** A wallboard made of dry plaster sandwiched between layers of cardboard.

> **plasterboard.** Same as sheetrock.

> **drywall construction.** Use of sheetrock or other pre-made material to make the walls. The other way to build the walls is to use wet plaster.

Questions

1. Sheetrock.

__ **A.** dry plaster

__ **B.** wet plaster

2. Match.

__ the walls   **A.** conduits

__ inside the walls   **B.** plasterboard

3. You nail the plasterboard to —

__ **A.** conduits

__ **B.** studs

4. Carries wiring or pipes.

__ **A.** lines

__ **B.** studs

5. Match.

__ plasterboard   **A.** sheetrock

__ wood timbers   **B.** frame

6. Drywall construction.

__ **A.** plaster it, let it dry

__ **B.** use plasterboard

◆

Many builders construct *prefab* or *modular* housing.

> **prefab.** Short for "prefabricated," which means "made ahead of time." A prefab house is made of parts that are cut out and prepared at the factory. The parts are put together into a house by the builder.

> **modular.** A modular house is one kind of prefab house. It is designed in sections, called "modules." The person putting up the house chooses which modules to use.

Questions

1. What do you think is the main reason for using prefab parts?

__ **A.** bigger

__ **B.** cheaper

__ **C.** one of a kind

2. In order for you to have a choice of which modular parts to use, the parts have to fit well together.

__ True   __ False

Chapter Review

1. Match.

__ means made at a factory

__ made of sheetrock

__ hold the walls

__ carry electrical or plumbing lines

    A. conduits

    B. drywall

    C. prefab

    D. studs

2. Match.

__ made so parts fit together

__ means same as sheetrock

__ passed a test (as with electricians or plumbers)

    A. modular

    B. plaster-board

    C. licensed

3. Match.

__ basement

__ made of timbers

__ place to build

    A. foundation

    B. frame

    C. site

4. Match.

__ to level

__ to restore

__ to tear down

    A. demolition

    B. grading

    C. renovation

5. Match.

__ learning job

__ skilled worker

    A. apprentice

    B. journey-man

6. Match.

__ joins metal pieces

__ machine with long neck

__ works with brick or stone

__ works with wires

    A. crane

    B. electrician

    C. mason

    D. welder

7. Match.

__ builds for others

__ builds big projects

    A. contractor

    B. developer

8. Match.

__ bridges and roads

__ frame houses

    A. light con-struction

    B. heavy construction

9. Match.

__ from person to person and machine to machine

__ factory

__ moving belt

__ wooden platform

    A. assembly line

    B. conveyor

    C. pallet

    D. plant

10. Match.

__ often has engine, lifts up pallets

__ platform on 4 wheels

__ same as pallet

__ stack boxes on it, push it like a wheelbarrow

    A. dolly

    B. fork lift

    C. hand truck

    D. skid

11. Match.

___ boss   **A.** assembler

___ gets boxes ready   **B.** foreman
to be shipped   **C.** packer

___ puts parts of products
together

12. Match.

___ boss   **A.** adjuster

___ skilled operator   **B.** machinist

___ "sets up" machine for   **C.** supervisor
new job

13. Match.

___ keeping machines   **A.** down time
in order
         B. jam

___ making sure the   **C.** maintenance
products are OK
         D. quality
___ tells you how to   control
do the job
         E. specs
___ things get stuck

___ when the machine is
not running

14. Match.

___ almost exactly to per-   **A.** blueprints
fect size
         B. close
___ science of making   tolerances
machines do jobs hu-
mans have always   **C.** robotics
done

___ type of specs

5

PRINTING, ELECTRONICS, AND PLASTICS — THREE BASIC INDUSTRIES

Words in this chapter:

offset printing
offset lithography
printing press
2-color and 4-color presses
negative
camera-ready copy
mechanical
printing plate
prep department
bindery
components
vacuum tube
miniaturized
printed circuit board (PC board)
transistor

solid state
integrated circuit (IC)
chip
polyurethane
polystyrene
styrofoam
film
shrink-wrapping
mold
injection molding
cavity
vacuum forming
extrusion
tool
die

A Printing

Almost any employer you work for is likely to need a lot of printing. Most printing today is **offset printing,** or **offset lithography.** A big offset printing plant may have several big expensive **presses.** It may have **2-color** and **4-color presses.** Some of the modern presses are run partly by computers.

offset printing. In offset printing, ink is first put onto the smooth rollers of the press (see below). The ink then is transferred to the paper as it goes around the rollers. An older kind of printing, where the ink is printed directly on the paper, is called "letterpress."

offset lithography. Another name for offset printing (called "offset litho" for short).

printing press. A printing machine.

2-color and **4-color presses.** A 2-color press prints two different colors in the same pass of the paper through the machine. A 4-color press prints four colors at once. By mixing colors it can print pictures that look like color photos.

Questions

1. The definition of offset printing explains —

__ **A.** how big the print is

__ **B.** how ink goes on the paper

__ **C.** how many pages are in the book

2. Match.

__ most printing in 1924   **A.** letterpress

__ most printing nowadays   **B.** offset

3. Match.

__ machine   **A.** lithography

__ type of printing   **B.** press

4. Do you think a printed page with black letters and a red border is 2-color printing?

__ yes   __ no

5. The cover of this book was printed with 4 colors. Can you pick them out? (You don't have to write down any answer for this question.)

6. Can you find anything else in the room you're in now that is printed with 4 colors, perhaps something with a color picture that looks like a color photo?

Describe one such item.

_____

_____

In offset printing you shoot *negatives* of *camera-ready copy* or of *mechanicals.* Then the negatives are used to make *printing plates.*

negative. A part of the film process in photography. When you take a black-and-white photo with your camera you get a "negative" which can then be used to make the finished picture. A printing negative is used to make the *printing plate* (see below).

camera-ready copy. In printing, the word "copy" means anything you are going to print. "Camera-ready copy" is copy that is ready to be photographed by the printer to make a negative. The negative will then be used to make a printing plate. Camera-ready copy can be anything from a simple typed page to a complex mechanical (see below).

mechanical. Copy that an artist pastes up on a piece of cardboard so that everything is in the correct position on the page. A mechanical may contain words, headlines, illustrations, etc. A finished mechanical may be used as camera-ready copy.

printing plate. A sheet of metal or even paper containing the image of what is to be printed. You put the plate into the press and ink goes onto the image. The inked image is what is printed.

Questions

1. Ink is printed on the paper from the —

__ **A.** negative

__ **B.** plate

2. How do you get a printing negative?

__ **A.** draw it

__ **B.** take a photo

__ **C.** type it

3. Which comes first?

__ **A.** mechanical

__ **B.** negative

__ **C.** plate

4. Match.

__ art or type   **A.** mechanical

__ goes on press   **B.** negative

__ photographic   **C.** plate

5. What makes copy "camera-ready"?

__ **A.** goes inside the press

__ **B.** made from a negative

__ **C.** ready to be photographed

A printing plant may have a *prep department.* It may also have its own *bindery.*

prep department. Takes pictures of what is to be printed and then in turn uses the negatives to make the printing plates that go on the press.

bindery. Takes the printed sheets and makes them into the finished product. If the finished product is a book, the bindery will fold the pages, "trim" them (cut them) to size, and "bind" them (to hold them together).

Questions

1. "Prep" in "prep department" is short for —

__ **A.** preparation

__ **B.** prepayment

__ **C.** preposition

2. Match.

__ gets ready for the print job

__ finishes the print job

A. bindery

B. prep department

3. Match.

__ work with mechanicals and negatives

__ work with folding and cutting machines

A. bindery

B. prep department

B Electronics

Like printing, electronics has become common in all parts of the world of work. It doesn't make any difference what your job is. Everywhere you're likely to use electronic devices.

Until the 1950's, electronic devices such as radios and TV's had to be large because their **components** were large. **Vacuum tubes** took up a lot of space. So did the other components.

> **components.** Parts. Electronic parts in particular are often referred to as components.
>
> **vacuum tube.** Radio tube that looks a little like a light bulb. It has wires inside a glass top. The bottom fits into a plug. Air is drawn out of the glass to leave a vacuum, because air hinders the flow of electricity. The one kind of vacuum tube that is still common is the TV tube on which we watch TV.

Questions

1. Match.

___ vacuum   **A.** container

___ tube   **B.** no air

2. If you've looked inside a radio or TV, you may have seen all sorts of little tube-shaped parts with wires coming out of each end. The tube-shaped centers are painted with bands of color.

   Do you think these are components?

   ___ yes   ___ no

◆

Today, electronic components are **miniaturized**. **Printed circuit boards** replace the old tangle of wires in an electronic device.

> **miniaturized.** Made very small. Hand-held radios and hand-held cassette recorders are miniaturized electronic devices.
>
> **printed circuit board.** A board on which an electronic circuit is "printed" in metal "ink." The electric current flows along the metal lines, in and out of miniaturized components. Called "PC board" for short.

Questions

1. Match.

___ old   **A.** printed circuit board

___ new   **B.** vacuum tube

2. "Miniaturized" describes —

   ___ **A.** beauty

   ___ **B.** size

   ___ **C.** strength

3. Match.

__ metal on a board   **A.** PC

__ no air   **B.** vacuum

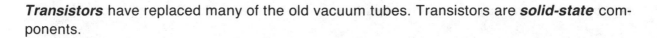

Transistors have replaced many of the old vacuum tubes. Transistors are ***solid-state*** components.

> **transistor.** A miniaturized component that acts as a kind of electronic switch. It can turn current on or off. One kind can make a weak electric "signal" stronger, a job many old vacuum tubes used to do.

> **solid state.** A solid-state component is made of several different solid layers of materials. These miniaturized layers can do the same jobs as the old vacuum tubes.

Questions

1. Match.

__ bigger and more expensive   **A.** transistor

__ smaller and cheaper   **B.** vacuum tube

2. Solid-state component.

__ **A.** miniaturized

__ **B.** old and big

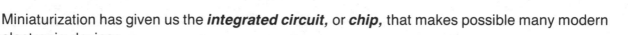

Miniaturization has given us the ***integrated circuit,*** or ***chip,*** that makes possible many modern electronic devices.

> **integrated circuit.** Solid-state device where many different circuits, transistors, and other components have all been put together on a tiny piece of material. You need a microscope to see everything on it. Called "IC" for short.

> **chip.** Another name for an IC because it's made of a small chip of material. Some of the different kinds of chips can be used as the brains of computers. That's why modern computers don't have to be very large. Chips are also used to do complex things in all sorts of other devices, from toys to large machines.

Questions

1. Match.

__ IC   **A.** metal lines on a board

__ PC   **B.** tiny layers

2. Match.

__ miniaturized switch   **A.** chip

__ several circuits and components all in one   **B.** transistor

Review

1. Match.

___ offset litho   **A.** offset printing

___ press   **B.** printing machine

2. Goes on the press.

___ **A.** camera-ready copy

___ **B.** mechanical

___ **C.** negative

___ **D.** plate

3. Makes into finished book

___ **A.** prep department

___ **B.** bindery

4. "Miniaturized" means "made very
_____ ."

5. PC board.

___ **A.** electric current flows along metal lines

___ **B.** made like a sandwich, with layers of components

6. Transistor.

___ **A.** glass vacuum tube

___ **B.** miniature switch

7. Chip.

___ **A.** integrated circuit

___ **B.** PC board

C Plastics

Plastics is a third industry that supplies businesses throughout the world of work.

Did you ever think of how many things in our modern world are made of plastic? **Polyurethane, polystyrene,** and **polystyrene** foam (or "**styrofoam**") are only a few of the common types of plastic. All of them are used frequently in the world of work.

polyurethane. A common kind of plastic with many uses. As a liquid you brush it onto wood floors, where it dries to form a hard, tough surface. Another kind of polyurethane makes "foam rubber." Still another kind is used as insulation inside the walls of houses.

polystyrene. A hard, inexpensive plastic. You can use it for throwaway plastic dishes and drinking cups. It's also used in toys. Polystyrene foam is the stiff, very light white plastic you use inside boxes to protect such things as radios and TV's and even big things such as refrigerators.

styrofoam. Polystyrene foam.

Questions

1. Match.

__ hard, light **A.** polyurethane foam

__ soft, rubbery **B.** polystyrene foam

2. Protection for wood.

__ **A.** polyurethane

__ **B.** polystyrene

3. "Styro-," in "styrofoam."

__ **A.** comes from styrene

__ **B.** comes from urethane

One of the important uses of plastic in industry is for *film* for *shrink-wrapping.*

film. As used in *shrink-wrapping* (see below), a very thin sheet of clear plastic which comes in rolls.

shrink-wrapping. A way of protecting packages. You put the package inside a loose film envelope. Then you seal the ends by means of heat and pass the package through a heated machine. The heat shrinks the film and makes it fit tight. Shrink-wrapping is used to protect records, toys in boxes, and many, many other products, including some of the things you are likely to work with on the job.

Questions

1. "Film," as used above.

__ **A.** for cameras

__ **B.** for movies

__ **C.** for packaging

2. Shrink-wrapping.

__ **A.** shrinks to curl up

__ **B.** shrinks to fit tight

__ **C.** shrinks to make lighter

3. What makes the film shrink?

__ **A.** electricity

__ **B.** heat

__ **C.** water

Plastics are shaped in many different ways. To make solid plastic objects you usually use *molds* by means of *injection molding.* You often use a mold with many *cavities* so that many parts can be made at one time.

mold. A hollow object you use to shape things. For example, an ice tray is a mold you use to make ice cubes.

injection molding. A way of shaping plastic inside a hollow mold. The hollows in the mold have the shape you want the final parts to be. Melted plastic is forced through small openings into the mold until the mold is filled. The plastic hardens and takes on the shape of the mold.

cavity. Hollow space inside a mold.

Questions

1. Injection molding.

__ **A.** to heat plastic

__ **B.** to shape plastic

__ **C.** to strengthen plastic

2. Mold.

__ **A.** plastic goes inside

__ **B.** plastic goes outside

3. "Cavity," as used here.

__ **A.** hole inside a mountain

__ **B.** part of a mold

__ **C.** problem with teeth

Two other common methods of shaping plastic are **vacuum forming** and **extrusion.** You use vacuum forming to shape thin pieces of plastic, such as the "bubbles" of clear plastic sometimes used to protect items packaged on a card. You use extrusion to shape tubes or other long pieces of plastic.

vacuum forming. In vacuum forming you lay a sheet of heated plastic on top of a solid form. A "vacuum" sucks the sheet down over the form so that it takes on the shape of the form. When the sheet cools, the new shape is permanent.

extrusion. In extrusion, melted plastic is squeezed out of a machine like toothpaste from a toothpaste tube. When cool, the plastic keeps its squeezed-out shape.

Questions

1. Match.

__ vacuum forming   **A.** electronics

__ vacuum tube   **B.** plastics

2. Match.

__ force plastic into cavities   **A.** extrusion

__ squeeze it into the shape you want it   **B.** injection molding

__ suck sheets down over form   **C.** vacuum forming

3. Match.

__ plastic bubble   **A.** shrink-wrap

__ heat it to make it fit tight   **B.** vacuum form

One reason plastic is used so widely in our modern world is that the cost of the plastic is fairly cheap. But the costs of the *tools* and *dies* can be expensive.

tool. In the plastics business, another name for a mold.

die. A word with 2 meanings in the plastics business. In extrusion, a die is a machine part with a hole in it that the plastic is squeezed through. The die gives the extrusion its shape. In vacuum forming, a die is a device that works like a cookie cutter to cut out the plastic part from the plastic sheet once it has cooled.

Questions

1. What are tools and dies used for in plastics?

__ **A.** to cool the plastic

__ **B.** to heat the plastic

__ **C.** to shape the plastic

2. Plastics tools have cavities.

__ True   __ False

3. Match.

__ cutter   **A.** die in extrusion

__ hole   **B.** die in vacuum forming

Chapter Review

1. Match.

___ letterpress   A. old method

___ offset printing   B. new method

2. Match.

___ camera-ready   A. goes on press
     copy   B. photographic film

___ negative   C. sometimes a typed

___ plate   page, sometimes
                            a mechanical

3. Match.

___ binding   A. get ready for
                        printing

___ prep   B. printing machine

___ press   C. cut, fold, and stitch
                       or glue

4. Miniaturized, in electronics.

___ A. in 1940

___ B. today

5. Match.

___ IC   A. chip

___ PC   B. like light bulb

___ transistor   C. uses metal lines

___ vacuum tube   D. solid state elec-
                     tronic switch

6. Match.

___ film for negatives, to   A. plastics
     make plates   B. printing

___ film for shrink-wrapping

7. Match.

___ polystyrene foam   A. film that
                            fits tight over
___ shrink-wrap   boxes

___ vacuum forming   B. for "bub-
                            ble" package

                            C. for hard
                            white plastic
                            packing
                            material

8. Match.

___ foam rubber and wood   A. polystyrene
     floor surface   B. polyure-
___ styrofoam and plastic   thane
     cups

9. Match.

___ force it into cavities   A. extrusion

___ squeeze it out   B. injection
                          molding

10. Match.

___ cavity   A. cutter or
                     hole
___ die

___ tool   B. mold

                     C. hollow
                     space in mold

6
UNIONS

Words in this chapter:

union member
waiting period
union card
initiation fee
open shop
union shop
dues checkoff
seniority
layoff
hiring hall
shapeup
labor
management
negotiate
union contract

collective bargaining
job action
strike
picket line
NLRB
cooling off period
wildcat strike
lockout
wages
pension fund
job security
grievance
grievance procedure
shop steward
local

A Membership

The place where you get a job may have a union. You may want to join. But it's possible you won't be able to become a *union member* right away. There may be a *waiting period* before you can get your *union card.* In some types of unions there will be an *initiation fee.*

union member. Person who belongs to a union. You pay dues, but you get many different kinds of benefits.

waiting period. A typical waiting period is 30 to 60 days from the time you're hired until you can get into the union.

union card. A card that shows you are in the union. Each union member has a card with a different number.

initiation fee. Fee for being allowed to join the union.

Questions

1. Jaime started a new job on August 6. He wanted to join the union, but he had to wait until September 15.

   The time from August 6 to September 15 was a _____ _____.

2. Jaime had to pay $6 per week from his salary as union dues. In return, here are some of the benefits he got:

* *Membership in a union health program with free medical care.*

* *Membership in a program which will give him money when he retires, provided he stays in the union long enough.*

* *The union will try to get him and its other members higher pay and protection against getting fired.*

* *The union will back him up if he has good reason to complain about working conditions or the way the bosses are treating him.*

   Do you think the union is a good deal for Jaime? (There is no right or wrong answer here. The question just asks your opinion.)

   __ Yes   __ No

3. Union card.

   __ **A.** every member gets one
   __ **B.** it's a list of all the members in the union

4. What do you think *initiation* means?

   __ **A.** beginning
   __ **B.** end

If there is an **open shop** you can decide whether or not you want to join the union. But if there is a **union shop,** you won't have any choice. Either way, if you join, you may pay your dues by means of a **dues checkoff.**

> **open shop.** A company that employs both union and non-union members.

> **union shop.** Everyone who joins the company as a worker has to join the union too.

> **dues checkoff.** Your union dues are automatically taken out of your paycheck by the company.

Questions

1. Match.

__ you can join if you want **A.** open shop

__ you have to join **B.** union shop

2. Match.

__ company wants it **A.** union shop

__ union wants it **B.** open shop

3. If you have a dues checkoff, whose money pays the dues?

__ **A.** company's money

__ **B.** your money

4. With a dues checkoff you can take as long as you want to pay your dues.

__ True __ False

How long you have been a union member determines your **seniority.** This can be particularly important if there is a **layoff.**

> **seniority.** The people with the highest seniority are those who have been members longest. Or in some cases, the people who have been working for the company the longest.

> **layoff.** Temporarily losing your job. When a company with a union lays off a number of workers it does so by seniority. The people with the least seniority get laid off first. The people with the highest seniority keep their jobs the longest.

Questions

1. Marie has been working on the job as a union member for 12 years. Elaine has been at the same job, also as a union member, for 7 years.

   Who has higher seniority?

   __ **A.** Marie

   __ **B.** Elaine

2. If business gets bad, who will be in danger of being laid off first?

   __ **A.** Marie

   __ **B.** Elaine

In some industries, the union actually does the hiring. It might have a *hiring hall.* It might hire by means of a *shapeup.*

> **hiring hall.** A union hall where the union hires members for jobs in the companies it deals with. The seamen's unions have hiring halls to hire members for jobs on ships.

> **shapeup.** In a shapeup, the members who want the jobs that have been announced give notice that they are available. In some cases, they simply step forward. In other cases, they pass in their union cards. The union represenstive will then pick the members who get the jobs, usually by seniority.

Questions

1. In a union hiring hall, who decides what members get the jobs?

   __ **A.** representative of company

   __ **B.** representative of union

2. What do you do when you "shape up" for a job?

   __ **A.** show you want it

   __ **B.** sign your name

   __ **C.** do a lot of running

B What Unions Do

The goals of *labor* are not always the same as the goals of *management.*

> **labor.** The workers. The term "labor" usually refers to workers who are in a union.

> **management.** The people who manage a business. Management will want to make profits, while labor will want higher pay and better working conditions.

Question

1. Miss Giordano is a representative of the union. Mrs. Ottavio is a vice president of the company.

   Match.

   ___ Miss Giordano   **A.** labor

   ___ Mrs. Ottavio   **B.** management

◆

The union and management *negotiate* a *union contract.* Then the members vote to decide whether they will accept it. This is all part of *collective bargaining.*

> **negotiate.** To bargain.

> **union contract.** The legal document that spells out how the company is to treat the union and its members. Typical union contracts are only good for one year or a few years. Then a new contract has to be negotiated.

> **collective bargaining.** Negotiation by the union with management. The union bargains for the benefit of the "collective" membership, that is, for the whole group of members.

Questions

1. Match.

___ try to work out a deal   **A.** negotiate

___ the members have the   **B.** vote
    final say

2. Union contract.

___ **A.** between the company and the union

___ **B.** between you and the union

3. "Collective" in "collective bargaining."

___ **A.** bosses

___ **B.** union members

If the union and management can't work out a contract, there may be a *job action* or a *strike.* If there is a strike, the union members will go on the *picket line.*

    job action. Such things as a slowdown of work, or a lot of workers calling in sick, or a *picket line* (see below) by the workers after they get off work each day.

    strike. Refusal to go to work. The union may have a "strike fund" to give money to members who lose their pay when they're out on strike.

    picket line. A line of union members who march up and down in front of the company they are on strike against. People on a picket line carry signs which explain the union's position. They will try to convince people not to "cross the picket line," that is, not to go inside the company's place of business.

Questions

1. The machine operators in a particular company have decided a new job rule is unfair. To protest they refuse to do anything at all that is not spelled out in the contract as part of their job. This leads to work getting done much slower than usual.

___ **A.** job action

___ **B.** strike

2. Next Tuesday, unless they get a new contract, all the union members in a particular company are going to stay out of work.

___ **A.** job action

___ **B.** strike

3. People on a picket line.

___ **A.** bosses

___ **B.** union members

4. Match.

___ temporarily lose your job   **A.** layoff

___ refuse to go to work   **B.** strike

If there is a threat of a strike, the **NLRB** may step in and ask for a *cooling off period.*

NLRB. Short for **N**ational **L**abor **R**elations **B**oard. The NLRB is set up by the federal government to oversee the way unions and companies deal with each other. States and local governments also have labor relations boards.

cooling off period. Delay in a strike, for perhaps 80 days. The idea is that the two sides will have a chance to "cool off" their anger at each other. Then maybe they can negotiate a contract without a long, costly strike.

Questions

1. Match.

__ "N" in NLRB   **A.** federal government
__ "LR" in NLRB   **B.** the people in the government agency
__ "B" in NLRB
                              C. way workers and management get along

2. Cooling off period.

__ **A.** before the contract runs out
__ **B.** before a strike
__ **C.** before the workers go back to work

The union is not always able to control its workers and prevent *wildcat strikes.*

wildcat strike. A strike by a group of workers, *without* the OK of the union.

Question

1. The word "wildcat" in "wildcat strike."

__ **A.** big and furry
__ **B.** out of control

In a strike, the workers try to put pressure on the company by causing it to lose business.

At the same time, the workers lose wages. And sometimes companies try to put pressure on the workers by means of a *lockout.*

> **lockout.** An action taken by management to keep workers from going to work. Management will sometimes do this as an answer to a job action.

Questions

1. Lockout.

__ **A.** union members refuse to work

__ **B.** company won't let them go to work

2. "Lockout" and "strike" are —

__ **A.** opposite

__ **B.** the same

3. Match.

__ temporarily close a factory because business is bad

__ close a factory to put pressure on the union

A. layoff

B. lockout

◆

The tough points to work out in a union contract usually have to do with *wages,* the *pension fund,* and *job security.*

> **wages.** Pay.
>
> **pension fund.** Money used for benefits for workers who get old enough to retire. The union often manages the pension fund, as well as medical insurance programs. The workers may put in part of the money for the pension fund from their wages. The company will usually put in the rest. If you go to another job which has the same union, your pension program will stay the same.
>
> **job security.** Protection against losing your job.

Questions

1. A recent contract in a particular industry calls for an average $1.40 per hour increase in pay, more money for retirement benefits, and a guarantee that no plants will be closed down for 2 years.

Match.

___ $1.40 per hour   **A.** job security

___ more money for retire-   **B.** pension
     ment benefits   fund

___ no plant closings   **C.** wages

2. Who has better job security?

___ **A.** union member with low seniority

___ **B.** union member with high seniority

The union contract will also specify how *grievances* are to be handled. It will spell out a whole *grievance procedure.*

> **grievance.** A complaint of a worker, usually about working conditions or the violation of a rule in the contract.

> **grievance procedure.** How the grievance is to be handled. How and where you present it, who is supposed to make a decision, the rules for making that decision, your right to appeal if the decision goes against you — and so on.

Questions

1. Helen is a skilled machine operator and a union member. Her boss moved her into a job packing boxes and reduced her pay.

Do you think this is the type of the thing that might be considered a grievance?

___ yes   ___ no

2. How is the best way for Helen to handle her problem?

___ **A.** follow the grievance procedure in the contract

___ **B.** organize a strike

___ **C.** quit

The *shop steward* is an important person in the grievance procedure. In fact, the shop steward is a key person in all the affairs of the *local.*

> **shop steward.** A union member who represents a small group of fellow members in their union affairs and their dealings with management (such as in a grievance). Shop stewards are elected by the group. They often keep their regular jobs while at the same time working on union business.

> **local.** The local branch of a union.

Questions

1. Local, as used above.

__ **A.** train

__ **B.** crazy

__ **C.** part

2. Shop steward.

__ **A.** company supervisor

__ **B.** represents the union members

3. Shop steward.

__ **A.** chosen by company president

__ **B.** chosen by union members

4. The main headquarters for Martha's union is in Chicago. The part that represents members in Martha's area is in Columbus.

Martha's local.

__ **A.** Chicago

__ **B.** Columbus

5. Match.

__ shop foreman (from an earlier chapter)   **A.** company job

__ shop steward   **B.** union job

Chapter Review

1. Match.

___ representatives of the company   **A.** labor

___ representatives of the union   **B.** management

___ representatives of the government   **C.** NLRB

2. Match.

___ how a complaint is to be handled   **A.** collective bargaining

___ negotiation on behalf of the union members   **B.** grievance procedure

3. Match.

___ before a strike   **A.** cooling off period

___ before you can get your union card   **B.** waiting period

4. Match.

___ you don't have to join   **A.** union shop

___ you have to join   **B.** open shop

5. Match.

___ elected by the members   **A.** shapeup

___ negotiated by union representatives, voted on by members   **B.** shop steward

___ union representative makes the choice   **C.** union contract

6. Match.

___ complaint   **A.** grievance

___ how long you've been a union member   **B.** job security

___ protection against losing your job   **C.** seniority

7. Match.

___ branch of a union   **A.** hiring hall

___ where representatives of the union select members for jobs in companies the union deals with   **B.** local

8. Match.

___ you pay it when you join the union   **A.** dues checkoff

___ the company takes it out of your wages automatically   **B.** initiation fee

___ pays you money when you retire   **C.** pension fund

9. Match.

___ slowdown of work   **A.** layoff

___ union tells its members not to go to work   **B.** lockout

___ group of workers refuses to go to work, even though union hasn't called a strike   **C.** job action

___ temporary loss of jobs because business is bad   **D.** strike

___ company keeps workers away from their jobs to put pressure on union   **E.** wildcat strike

7

PAY, TAXES, AND INSURANCE

Words in this chapter:

wages
salary
hourly pay
weekly pay
piecework
time sheet
time clock
biweekly
bimonthly
semimonthly
time-and-a-half
overtime
double time
compensatory time off
benefits
fringe benefits
pension plan
profit sharing plan
bonus
expense account
per diem expenses
reimburse
sick leave
personal days
leave of absence
W-4 form
IRS

allowance
income taxes
withholding taxes
exempt
FICA
W-2 form
file tax returns
short form
itemize deductions
joint return
capital gains tax
tax rate
tax bracket
Blue Cross
major medical
fee-for-service
group medical insurance
contribution
claim form
deductible
exclusion
unemployment insurance
workmen's compensation
disability
group life
the insured
beneficiary

A Pay

How are your **wages** paid? Do you get a **weekly salary?** Or are you paid on an **hourly** or **piecework** basis?

wages. Pay.

salary. Regular pay. How much you get for an hour of work or for a week on a regular basis.

hourly pay. Set amount of pay for each hour of work.

weekly pay. Pay for a week of work.

piecework. Pay based on how many items of a particular kind you produce.

Questions

1. Mark makes $155 per week. Last week he worked extra hours, so that his pay before taxes came to $172.50.

   Match.

   __ $155   **A.** regular pay

   __ $172.50   **B.** total wages for week

2. Sam is a machine operator. His paycheck for last week showed he earns $7 per hour and that he worked 32 hours for total earnings of $224. The paycheck of his boss, Anita, just shows she earned $340 for the week, which is her regular pay.

   Match.

   __ Sam   **A.** paid on hourly basis

   __ Anita   **B.** paid on weekly basis

3. Match.

   __ 40 cents per item you produce   **A.** hourly pay

   __ $5 per hour you work   **B.** piecework

If you are paid hourly you may have to fill out *time sheets* or punch a *time clock.*

time sheet. A form you fill out. Tells what time you got to work each day, what time you left, and how many hours you worked.

time clock. You push a card into a time clock and it punches the time you went to work. Then at the end of the day you push the card in again and it punches the time you left work.

Questions

1. Match.

___ fill it in and sign   **A.** time clock

___ push the card in   **B.** time sheet
("punch" it)

2. What's the purpose of time sheets and time clocks? (Answer in your own words.)

_____

_____

◆

Some workers get paid at the end of every day they work. Most people get paid weekly or *biweekly* (or *bimonthly,* that is, *semimonthly*).

biweekly. Every 2 weeks.

bimonthly. Usually means twice a month, as, for example, the 1st and 15th of the month. (However, it can mean every 2 months — a very confusing term.)

semimonthly. Twice per month, same as the first meaning of bimonthly.

Questions

1. Get paid on the 15th and 30th of every month.
   - __ **A.** weekly
   - __ **B.** biweekly
   - __ **C.** bimonthly

2. Get paid every Friday.
   - __ **A.** weekly
   - __ **B.** biweekly
   - __ **C.** bimonthly

3. Get paid every second Friday.
   - __ **A.** weekly
   - __ **B.** biweekly
   - __ **C.** bimonthly

4. Match.
   - __ biweekly
   - __ semimonthly

   A. every 2 weeks

   B. same as one meaning of bimonthly

5. Match.
   - __ 2 paychecks in 28 days
   - __ 2 paychecks in 30 days (or 31 days, depending on the month)

   A. biweekly

   B. semi-monthly

◆

Some jobs pay *time-and-a-half* for *overtime* and *double time* for work on Sunday. Other companies give *compensatory time off.*

time-and-a-half. 1½ times your regular pay. If you regularly make $5 per hour, you make $7.50 per hour at time-and-a-half. Time-and-a-half is often paid for *overtime* hours (see below).

overtime. Extra time worked on a particular day or in a particular week. In most jobs you are expected to work either 7 or 8 hours per day and a total of either 35 or 40 hours per week. If you are only expected to work 8 hours per day and you work 10 hours on a particular day, you earn 2 hours of overtime pay.

double time. Twice your regular pay, often for hours worked on Sunday.

compensatory time off. An equal amount of time off for overtime hours worked. If you work 2 hours of overtime and you get compensatory time off, you are entitled to take 2 hours off.

Questions

1. Rita is expected to work 35 hours per week on her job. Last week she worked 39 hours.

   How many overtime hours did she work?

   _____

2. Rita's regular pay is $6 per hour.

   How much does she earn per hour at time-and-a-half? _____

3. In "compensatory time off," which word tells you that it's equal?

   __ **A.** compensatory

   __ **B.** time

   __ **C.** off

4. Compensatory time off is given by some employers for —

   __ **A.** regular hours worked

   __ **B.** extra hours worked

5. Two weeks ago, Rita worked Saturday and Sunday, in addition to her regular 5 days per week. Her company pays time-and-a-half and double time.

   Match.

   __ Saturday   **A.** time-and-a-half

   __ Sunday   **B.** double time

◆

In addition to your pay, you receive **benefits** (or **"fringe" benefits**). For example, you will probably get a paid vacation. Your employer may have a **pension plan.** Some employers have a **profit sharing plan** or pay some other kind of **bonus** at the end of the year.

benefits. Things of value you receive on the job in addition to your regular pay. Almost every worker gets paid vacations and holidays. Other possible benefits include free insurance and the things listed below.

fringe benefits. Same as benefits.

pension plan. Money paid into a fund to help you when you get old and retire. As you have seen, unions sometimes run the pension plan.

profit sharing plan. At the end of the year, each person gets an extra amount of pay as a share of the profits of the company.

bonus. Extra pay.

Questions

1. Extra week's pay for getting a big job done on time.

   __ **A.** pension

   __ **B.** profit sharing

   __ **C.** bonus

2. Margie retired at age 65. She gets $309 per month from the company's —

   __ **A.** pension plan

   __ **B.** profit sharing plan

   __ **C.** bonus

3. If AC-DC Electronics earns money for the year it gives part of the money to its employees.

___ **A.** pension

___ **B.** profit sharing

___ **C.** bonus

4. Which of the following are fringe benefits? (Check one or more.)

___ **A.** company pays for membership of employees in a health club

___ **B.** bonus at Christmas time

___ **C.** salary of $800 per month

___ **D.** use of company car

If you do a lot of traveling for your employer you may have an ***expense account.*** Some companies pay you ***per diem expenses.*** Others ***reimburse*** you for your expenses.

expense account. You've seen this word before in the section on sales work. If you have an expense account you are entitled to get paid by your employer for certain types of expenses you have on the job. The usual types of expenses that are repaid are for entertainment of customers, use of a car, and other travel expenses. Sales people often have expense accounts.

per diem expenses (pronounced like per-DEE-um). A set amount for every day. For example, your employer may pay you $20 per day for your meals while you are traveling on company business.

reimburse. Repay. To get reimbursed for expenses, you are expected to keep track of what you spent, hold on to your receipts, and prepare a list of everything, usually on an expense account form.

Questions

1. The company pays for your meals while you're traveling on company business.

___ **A.** part of expense account

___ **B.** part of regular pay

2. Match.

___ 25 cents per mile you travel

___ $15 per day for car expenses

    A. per diem

    B. reimbursement

3. "Diem" means _____ .

4. Match.

___ get back what you spend

___ get set amount, no matter what you spend

    A. per diem

    B. reimbursement

5. When is it important for you to keep receipts?

___ **A.** when you are reimbursed for your expenses

___ **B.** when you are on a per diem basis

On most jobs you are entitled to a certain amount of *sick leave.* And of course you get vacations. Some employers give you *personal days.* If you need a lot of extra time off you might ask if you can have a *leave of absence.*

sick leave. Pay for the days you're out sick. Some employers allow you up to 8 or 10 days of sick leave per year (or more). Others allow one day off for a certain number of weeks worked, for example, one day for every 6 weeks worked.

personal days. Days you can take off for your own reasons, with pay. You may get 2 or 3 personal days in addition to your vacation and sick leave.

leave of absence. Allows you to take a certain amount of time off and still get your job back when you return. You don't get paid for the time spent on a leave of absence.

Questions

1. Match.

___ with pay   **A.** leave of absence

___ without pay   **B.** sick leave

2. Bertha's employer lets her take 2 days off per year, with pay, for whatever reasons she wants. These 2 days are in addition to her regular vacation. Bertha usually takes one day for Christmas shopping and another day for her daughter's birthday.

___ **A.** leave of absence

___ **B.** personal days

___ **C.** sick leave

3. What's the advantage of a leave of absence?

___ **A.** get paid for time you take off

___ **B.** get your job back

4. The purpose of sick leave is to protect you when you're sick. Employers don't like it when you use sick leave days to add to your vacation.

___ True   ___ False

Review

1. Match.

__ fixed amount by the day   **A.** per diem expenses

__ repayment for what you spent   **B.** reimbursement

2. Match.

__ every second Wednesday   **A.** biweekly

__ on the 1st and 15th of the month   **B.** bimonthly

3. Match.

__ bonus   **A.** benefit

__ piecework   **B.** for overtime

__ time-and-a-half   **C.** pay according to how much you produce

4. When you have a leave of absence, do you get paid for the time you're not working?

__ yes   __ no

5. Match.

__ compensatory   **A.** day

__ diem   **B.** equal

__ pension   **C.** for retirement

B Taxes

When you start a new job you fill out a **W-4 form.** The W-4 form is an **IRS** form. It asks you how many **allowances** you claim.

W-4 form. A form that looks like this.

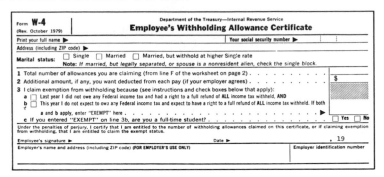

IRS. Short for **I**nternal **R**evenue **S**ervice — the part of the U.S. Government in charge of collecting taxes.

allowances. What you are allowed. On a W-4 form, each allowance is a set amount of money that does not have to be taken out of each paycheck for taxes. You get an allowance for each person you support, including yourself. You can get extra allowances for such things as being blind or being over 65 years of age.

Questions

1. Which word in "Internal Revenue Service" refers to the money it collects?

___ **A.** Internal

___ **B.** Revenue

___ **C.** Service

2. Andrew supports his father and 2 children.

How many dependents does he have?

_____

3. Andrew's total allowances are himself plus his dependents (answer to Question 2).

How many allowances can Andrew claim?

_____

4. Who fills out the part of the W-4 form that asks how many allowances you claim?

___ **A.** you do

___ **B.** your company does

◆

The W-4 form is a kind of **income tax** form. It figures out how much of your salary has to be set aside for **withholding taxes.**

income taxes. Taxes on the money you earn (your "income"). You have to pay **federal** income taxes to the U.S. government. In most states you have to pay **state** income taxes as well.

withholding taxes. Money taken out (or "withheld") from your paycheck for income taxes. Employers are responsible for withholding a part of your pay for taxes and sending it into the IRS (and to the state income tax department, if you pay state taxes).

Questions

1. When are withholding taxes taken out?

__ **A.** every paycheck

__ **B.** once per year

2. "Withhold" means —

__ **A.** hold forth

__ **B.** hold out

3. Which of the following is an income tax?

__ **A.** tax on a house you own

__ **B.** tax on your salary

__ **C.** tax on something you buy

Some people are *"exempt"* from withholding tax.

exempt. Not required. On a W-4 form, if you can claim you are exempt, you don't have to have any taxes withheld. You can claim to be exempt if you didn't pay any tax last year *and* if you don't expect to have to pay any this year.

Questions

1. Anne Marie is able to claim on the W-4 form that she is exempt.

This means that —

__ **A.** extra tax will be withheld

__ **B.** the regular tax will be withheld

__ **C.** no tax will be withheld

2. Match.

__ allowances   **A.** money held out

__ withholding taxes **B.** you and your dependents

Withholding taxes are not the only amounts taken out of your salary. Your employer also takes out for *FICA.*

FICA. Money for the Social Security Fund. (Stands for **F**ederal **I**nsurance **C**ontributions **A**ct — the law that set up Social Security.)

Question

1. Match.

___ for IRS   **A.** FICA

___ for Social Security **B.** withholding tax

At the end of the year, your employer will give you a ***W-2 form.*** When you ***file your tax returns*** you attach the W-2 form.

> **W-2 form.** Tells how much you earned during the year and how much taxes were withheld.

> **file tax returns.** Fill out and sign the tax form and send it into the government, along with a check for any extra money you owe. If the taxes withheld during the year from your taxes add up to more than your returns show you actually owe for the year, the IRS will send you a refund. If you pay both federal and state income taxes, you file returns with both the U.S. government and the state government. (You keep a copy of everything you file.)

Questions

1. Match.

___ every year   **A.** W-2 form

___ when you start job **B.** W-4 form

2. Margaret earned $12,807 last year. She had $2,130 withheld in federal taxes and $384 withheld in state taxes.

Which form will tell her this?

___ **A.** W-2

___ **B.** W-4

3. Match.

___ file   **A.** fill out, sign, and send

___ tax

___ return   **B.** money owed government

             C. the form

4. What do you do with the W-2 form?

___ **A.** give it to your employer

___ **B.** send it in with your tax returns and keep a copy

April 15 is the deadline for filing returns. If your taxes are simple you can use a **short form.** Otherwise, you'll want to **itemize deductions.**

short form. A simple tax form that makes it easy for you to fill in all the amounts and do the arithmetic.

itemize deductions. List in detail everything that will change the amount of taxes you owe. This is done on special forms. Such things as state taxes withheld, or heavy medical expenses, or money you lost in a business, or interest you paid on a loan can lower the amount of taxes you pay. You have to itemize each one of these "deductions" to get credit for them.

Questions

1. Why do some people itemize deductions?

___ **A.** saves money

___ **B.** saves time

2. Match.

___ itemize   **A.** list in detail

___ deductions   **B.** things that reduce your taxes

3. Jason's taxes are very simple. He doesn't have anything special to report that could change the amount of taxes he owes.

Should he use the short form?

___ yes   ___ no

If you're married you can file a **joint return.**

joint return. A tax return for husband and wife to file together, where incomes and deductions are combined.

Question

1. "Joint," as in "joint return."

___ **A.** for married couples

___ **B.** place to eat (with lousy food)

___ **C.** your elbow and ankles

If you made extra money from something other than your job, you'll pay taxes on this, too. For example, you may have a *capital gains tax.*

> **capital gains tax.** Tax for the profit you made on a property you sold. A capital gains tax is much less than the tax on the same amount of regular income. To take advantage of the lower capital gains tax, you have to hold the property for a certain amount of time before you sell it.

Questions

1. Last year, Cindy earned $25,000 in pay from her job. She also earned $25,000 in capital gains from the sale of some stocks and bonds.

   Match.

   __ higher tax amount **A.** her regular pay

   __ lower tax amount   **B.** her capital gains

2. Match.

   __ salary

   __ sale of building

   A. can be capital gains

   B. withholding tax

◆

Your *tax rate* depends on how much you earn. People who earn a lot of money are in a high *tax bracket.*

> **tax rate.** Percent of your income that you pay in taxes.

> **tax bracket.** The level of your tax rate. If your income increases enough, you will pay a higher tax rate. That is, you will go into a higher tax bracket.

Questions

1. Do people in a high tax bracket have a high tax rate?

   __ yes   __ no

2. Match.

   __ level

   __ percent

   A. bracket

   B. rate

◆

Review

1. Match.

___ FICA   **A.** income taxes

___ IRS   **B.** Social Security

2. Match.

___ W-2 form   **A.** fill it out when you start a job

___ W-4 form   **B.** shows how much you earned for year and how much tax was withheld

3. Match.

___ dependents   **A.** people you support

___ allowances   **B.** often yourself plus the people you support

4. How often are withholding taxes taken out?

___ **A.** every paycheck

___ **B.** on April 15

5. Match.

___ "file," in "file tax returns"   **A.** fill out and sign

___ "itemize," in "itemize deductions"   **B.** husband and wife

___ "joint," in "joint return"   **C.** list in detail

C Insurance

The most common type of medical insurance is **Blue Cross.** Some employers also carry **major medical insurance.** Some employers have a **fee-for-service** plan.

> **Blue Cross.** Pays basic hospital expenses. Blue Cross is a company. Other companies also offer hospitalization plans.
>
> **major medical.** Extra insurance often taken with a hospital plan. Pays at least a part of doctor fees, prescription drugs, and other medical fees, including some of the extra hospital fees not covered by your hospitalization plan.
>
> **fee-for-service.** Pays a certain amount every time you go to a doctor. If the doctor charges more, you pay the difference.

Questions

1. Sylvia got sick and had to go to the hospital. One of her company's medical plans paid the hospital bill of $960. The other medical plan paid 80% of the $416 it cost her for her doctor and medicine.

   Match.

   __ $960   **A.** Blue Cross
   __ 80% of $416   **B.** major medical

2. The ABC Company used to have a Blue Cross plan. Now it has medical insurance from another insurance company with a similar plan.

   __ **A.** fee-for-service
   __ **B.** hospital
   __ **C.** major medical

3. $15 for each visit to a doctor.

   __ **A.** fee-for-service
   __ **B.** hospital
   __ **C.** major medical

4. Blue Cross and other similar plans do **not** cover you for such things as a yearly visit to a doctor for a physical exam.

   __ True   __ False

◆

Group medical insurance costs less. Besides, the employer usually makes a **contribution.**

> **group medical insurance.** Coverage of a whole group of people, as for example, all the people working for a company.
>
> **contribution.** Payment of a part of the expense. Sometimes the employer pays half of the insurance costs and the employee pays half. Sometimes the employer pays the whole amount.

Questions

1. The company Cindy works for pays half of the cost of medical insurance for its employees. The total monthly cost for Cindy medical insurance is $18.

How much is the company's contribution?

__ $9

__ $18

__ $36

2. Is Cindy (Question 1 above) covered by a group medical insurance plan?

__ yes   __ no

3. If Cindy loses her job and decides to get the same medical insurance, but on her own individual plan, how much will she pay?

__ **A.** less than $18 a month

__ **B.** $18 a month

__ **C.** more than $18 a month

◆

Let's say you or one of your dependents gets sick and you have heavy medical expenses. If the sickness is covered by your insurance, you'll fill out a *claim form.* You may not get all of your expenses back. There may be a *deductible.* And there may be *exclusions.* And then the insurance company may only pay a certain percent of the rest of your expenses.

claim form. The doctor or hospital fills out part of it, your company may fill out part of it, and you fill out the rest. In some cases, the insurance pays the doctor or hospital directly. In other cases, you pay and then the insurance pays you back part or all of what you spent.

deductible. Amount subtracted from what the insurance company will pay. For example, you may have $100 per year deductible. Every year, you have to pay your first $100 of medical bills before the insurance company will start paying.

exclusion. Something the insurance company will **not** pay for.

Questions

1. Dependents are people whom you

   _____ .

2. Match.

   ___ does not pay first $300 per year of medical expenses for family

   ___ does not pay for the medical costs of having a baby

   A. deductible

   B. exclusion

3. You have filled out your part of a medical insurance claim form. The company has filled out its part.

   Who has to fill out the rest of the form?

   _____

4. Sean was *reimbursed* for his doctor expenses for an illness he had.

   ___ **A.** insurance company paid the doctor directly

   ___ **B.** Sean paid doctor and insurance company paid him back

5. "Claim," in "insurance claim form."

   ___ **A.** payment to insurance company

   ___ **B.** proof you were sick

   ___ **C.** request for payment

You are also covered on the job for 3 other kinds of insurance: *unemployment insurance, workmen's compensation,* and *disability.*

unemployment insurance. Pays you a certain amount of money each week if you get laid off from your job or are fired and can't get another job. To qualify for unemployment benefits, you have to have worked for a certain number of weeks. The company pays all or most of the costs of the insurance. In some states you pay a small amount, too. It's taken out of your paycheck.

workmen's compensation. Pays you a certain amount each week if you are injured ("disabled") on the job and can't go to work for a certain number of weeks. The reason for your being disabled has to be connected with work. Aside from an injury, the problem could be sickness, as, for example, getting sick from gas fumes. The company is required by law to carry this kind of insurance.

disability. Pays you a certain amount each wek when you can't go to work for a certain number of weeks because of a sickness or injury not caused by the job. The company pays all or most of the costs of this insurance. In some states you pay a small amount. The law requires employers to carry at least a minimium amount of disability insurance. Some companies will pay for extra disability insurance as a benefit for employees, so that if they are out of work with a long illness they will get even bigger disability payments — sometimes even as much as their regular pay.

Questions

1. Match.

___ box in warehouse falls and breaks foot, out of work 2 months

___ company goes out of business

___ has heart attack at home, out of work 4 months

    A. disability
    B. unemployment insurance
    C. workmen's compensation

2. Which word in "workmen's compensation" means "pay"?

___ **A.** workmen's

___ **B.** compensation

3. Match.

___ disability

___ workmen's compensation

    A. on job
    B. not on job

4. Who pays for most or all of the costs of unemployment insurance, workmen's compensation, and disability?

___ **A.** employer

___ **B.** employee

5. disabled

___ **A.** injured or sick

___ **B.** paid benefits

Your employer may also have a *group life* plan.

> **group life.** Life insurance, for a whole group of people. Because the insurance is for a whole group, the rates are lower. If you have a group life plan at work, the company may pay part or all of its insurance costs.

Question

1. Is life insurance for all the members of a union a group plan?

___ yes   ___ no

If you have a life insurance policy you are *the insured.* You have to name your *beneficiary.*

> **the insured.** The person who is insured. In family medical plans, the person who gets the insurance through the job is the insured, even though the other members of the family are also covered.

> **beneficiary.** In life insurance, the person who will receive the insurance benefits if you die.

Questions

1. Manola has life insurance. If she dies, the insurance money will go to her daughter.

   Match.

   __ Manola   **A.** beneficiary

   __ her daughter   **B.** the insured

2. Let's say you take out life insurance on yourself (you may already have it).

   Who would you want to be your beneficiary? _____

Chapter Review

1. Match.

___ Blue Cross

___ fee-for-service

___ major medical

A. covers at least part of the expenses the hospital plan doesn't

B. hospital insurance

C. set amount every time you go to the doctor

2. Match.

___ contribution

___ deductible

___ disability

___ exclusion

A. share of insurance fee paid (as by the company)

B. amount you have to pay before you start collecting insurance

C. insurance for when you're out sick for a long time

D. sickness the insurance doesn't cover

3. Person you name to collect the insurance.

___ **A.** beneficiary

___ **B.** the insured

4. Match.

___ group insurance

___ unemployment insurance

___ workmen's compensation

A. cheaper

B. for injury on the job

C. for when you get laid off

5. Match.

___ paid every Tuesday

___ paid every second Friday

___ paid 1st and 15th of month

A. bimonthly

B. biweekly

C. weekly

6. Match.

___ compensatory (as in "compensatory time off.")

___ piecework

___ time clock

___ time-and-a-half

A. equal

B. more than regular pay

C. pay according to what you produced

D. punch it

7. Match.

___ extra pay

___ money for travel and entertainment

___ money when you retire

A. bonus

B. expense account

C. pension

8. Match.

___ pay

___ profit-sharing plan

A. benefits

B. wages

9. Match.

___ pay per diem

___ reimburse

A. set amount

B. what you spent

10. Match.

___ leave of absence

___ personal days

A. with pay

B. without pay

11. Sick leave.

___ **A.** with pay

___ **B.** without pay

12. Match.

___ W-2 form

___ W-4 form

A. fill it out when you're hired

B. tells you what you earned and amount of taxes withheld

13. Match.

__ IRS   **A.** collects taxes

__ FICA   **B.** money for Social Security

14. Match.

__ allowance (on W-4)   **A.** every paycheck

__ exemption (on W-4)   **B.** percent

     C. you and your dependents

__ tax rate   **D.** not required

__ withholding tax

15. Match.

__ capital gains   **A.** for husband and wife

__ joint return   **B.** for sale of property

__ tax bracket   **C.** level

16. Match.

__ file tax returns   **A.** can save you money

__ itemize deductions   **B.** due April 15

__ use short form   **C.** easier to do